Deep Web Query Interface Understanding and Integration

Synthesis Lectures on Data Management

Editor
M. Tamer Özsu, *University of Waterloo*

Synthesis Lectures on Data Management is edited by Tamer Özsu of the University of Waterloo. The series will publish 50- to 125 page publications on topics pertaining to data management. The scope will largely follow the purview of premier information and computer science conferences, such as ACM SIGMOD, VLDB, ICDE, PODS, ICDT, and ACM KDD. Potential topics include, but not are limited to: query languages, database system architectures, transaction management, data warehousing, XML and databases, data stream systems, wide scale data distribution, multimedia data management, data mining, and related subjects.

Deep Web Query Interface Understanding and Integration
Eduard C. Dragut, Weiyi Meng, and Clement T. Yu
2012

P2P Techniques for Decentralized Applications
Esther Pacitti, Reza Akbarinia, and Manal El-Dick
2012

Query Answer Authentication
HweeHwa Pang and Kian-Lee Tan
2012

Declarative Networking
Boon Thau Loo and Wenchao Zhou
2012

Full-Text (Substring) Indexes in External Memory
Marina Barsky, Ulrike Stege, and Alex Thomo
2011

Spatial Data Management
Nikos Mamoulis
2011

Deep Web Query Interface Understanding and Integration

Eduard C. Dragut, Weiyi Meng, and Clement T. Yu

ISBN: 978-3-031-00761-3   paperback
ISBN: 978-3-031-01889-3   ebook

DOI 10.1007/978-3-031-01889-3

A Publication in the Springer series
SYNTHESIS LECTURES ON DATA MANAGEMENT

Lecture #26
Series Editor: M. Tamer Özsu, *University of Waterloo*
Series ISSN
Synthesis Lectures on Data Management
Print 2153-5418   Electronic 2153-5426

Deep Web Query Interface Understanding and Integration

Eduard C. Dragut
Purdue University

Weiyi Meng
Binghamton University

Clement T. Yu
University of Illinois at Chicago

SYNTHESIS LECTURES ON DATA MANAGEMENT #26

ABSTRACT

There are millions of searchable data sources on the Web and to a large extent their contents can only be reached through their own query interfaces. There is an enormous interest in making the data in these sources easily accessible. There are primarily two general approaches to achieve this objective. The first is to surface the contents of these sources from the deep Web and add the contents to the index of regular search engines. The second is to integrate the searching capabilities of these sources and support integrated access to them.

In this book, we introduce the state-of-the-art techniques for extracting, understanding, and integrating the query interfaces of deep Web data sources. These techniques are critical for producing an integrated query interface for each domain. The interface serves as the mediator for searching all data sources in the concerned domain. While query interface integration is only relevant for the deep Web integration approach, the extraction and understanding of query interfaces are critical for both deep Web exploration approaches.

This book aims to provide in-depth and comprehensive coverage of the key technologies needed to create high quality integrated query interfaces automatically. The following technical issues are discussed in detail in this book: query interface modeling, query interface extraction, query interface clustering, query interface matching, query interface attribute integration, and query interface integration.

KEYWORDS

Deep Web, Web database, query interface, query interface model, query interface extraction, query interface integration, attribute matching, attribute integration, query interface clustering

To Monica (wife) and to Alexia and Nicholas (children).

E.C.D.

To Xia (wife) and to Connie and Melissa (children).

W.M.

To Teresa (wife) and to Victor and Christine (children).

C.Y.

Contents

Preface

Most of the World Wide Web belongs to the so-called *deep Web*, which is the part of the Web whose contents are hidden behind the query interfaces of many search engines. In other words, deep Web contents can only be accessed through search engines. The deep Web itself can be further divided into two broad categories based on how well the data are structured. The first category contains data that have no or little structure, such as text documents (including HTML web pages), images, audio, and video. The second category contains data that have well-defined structures such as product records (e.g., books). Deep Web data sources of the second category are often known as *Web databases*. In this book, we focus on the query interfaces of Web databases.

The data in Web databases are usually stored in backend database systems. As the data are structured with clearly defined attributes, the query interfaces of Web databases often reflect some of these attributes to allow users to enter queries that can specify conditions on different attributes or fields. For example, for a book Web database, its query interface may allow users to specify search conditions on the fields *Title*, *Author*, *Subject*, and *ISBN*. Indeed, a significant difference between the query interfaces for Web databases and those for regular search engines that search text documents is that the former often has multiple input fields while the latter usually has a single input field (i.e., the textbox for entering search keywords).

In this book, we introduce technical issues related to processing the query interfaces of Web databases and we also summarize main representative techniques that have been proposed to tackle these issues. The issues include query interface representation (i.e., representing the information on a query interface using a representation model), query interface extraction (i.e., automatically extracting the representation information from query interfaces), query interface clustering and categorization (i.e., grouping query interfaces according to the domains of their Web database contents), query interface matching (i.e., matching semantically equivalent fields and attributes in different query interfaces), query interface attribute integration (i.e., integrating semantically equivalent attributes into a single attribute), and query interface integration (i.e., integrating multiple query interfaces in the same domain into an integrated query interface).

Query interface understanding and extraction are important for applications that need to interact with Web databases such as deep Web crawling (i.e., collecting the contents of Web databases through their query interfaces) and metasearching (i.e., querying multiple Web databases on the fly in a unified manner). Query interface integration aims to produce an integrated query interface for Web databases in the same domain. Obtaining such integrated query interfaces is an important step in building metasearch engines on top of Web databases such as comparison-shopping systems.

This book can be used as part of Web technology related courses such as Web data management. It can also be a reference book for IT professionals, especially researchers and developers in the Web database integration system area.

Eduard C. Dragut, Weiyi Meng, and Clement T. Yu
June 2012

Acknowledgments

We would like to express our deep gratitude to the series editor of the Synthesis Lectures on Data Management, Dr. M. Tamer Özsu, who read the entire manuscript carefully and provided very valuable and constructive suggestions which have helped improve the book significantly. We would also like to thank Can Lin for his input on the first chapter of the book. We are also grateful to the editor of the book, Diane Cerra, for her help and support in the course of preparing the book.

Eduard C. Dragut, Weiyi Meng, and Clement T. Yu
June 2012

CHAPTER 1

Introduction

The World Wide Web (simply referred to as the Web) is currently the largest information source in the world. In recent years, the Web has also become a major platform for business transactions. People from all walks of life use the Web to find needed information and conduct business activities on a regular basis. The Web has become an important part in many people's daily lives. Indeed, according to a recent report posted at the Internet World Stats[1], there were already over 2 billion Internet users by the end of March 2011.

The size of the Web has become so large that no one knows exactly how large it is. In 2005, Eric Schmidt, the former CEO of Google estimated the size of the Web to be about 5 million terabytes. Due to the fast growth of the Web, the current size of the Web should have become much larger. In contrast, the U.S. Library of Congress had archived about 235 terabytes of data as of April 2011[2], meaning that the Internet is at least 20,000 times larger than the archive of the U.S. Library of Congress. Another estimate is that the Web contains at least 1 trillion pages because even the portion, known as the *Deep Web* (see Section 1.1 for explanation), has about 1 trillion web pages in 2012 [Zillman, 2012].

To help ordinary users find desired information from the huge amount of data on the Web, many search engines have been created by researchers and developers in the Web community, and they have become the most popular tools for people to find desired information on the Web. There are different types of search engines. For example, some search engines are designed to search primarily web pages while others are designed to search structured records (e.g., books and airplane tickets). Search engines that search structured data are commonly called *Web databases* because the data they search are usually stored in database systems. In this book, we focus on Web databases, not search engines that are primarily designed to search web pages.

Each search engine on the Web has a query interface which allows users to submit queries based on their information needs. The query interfaces of Web databases are generally more complex than the typical query interfaces of search engines that search web pages. This is because the former often needs query conditions on different fields (e.g., need to specify *departing airport* and *arriving airport* when searching for flights) while the latter mostly just needs to support keywords based queries. In this book, we will focus on the query interfaces of Web databases. Indeed, the central focus of the book is to introduce techniques that deal with different aspects of the complex query interfaces of Web databases.

---

[1]http://www.internetworldstats.com/stats.htm. Accessed on December 10, 2011.
[2]http://www.loc.gov/webarchiving/faq.html#faqs_05. Accessed on December 10, 2011.

Most Web databases are domain specific. For example, most book search engines can only search books. Furthermore, no single Web database covers all data records, even for a single domain. For example, currently no single book search engine can search all books. There are various reasons for this situation. For example, some Web databases have restricted data sources (e.g., a publisher's search engine covers only the books it publishes) and some others may choose to be specialized (e.g., a search engine may choose to focus on computer science books only). The situation where no single Web database covers all materials, even for a specific domain, makes it very inconvenient for users. They may have to search many Web databases to find what they want. There is a genuine need to provide a way for users to find out what they want for each information need by submitting just one query. Different methodologies have been developed to achieve this objective. One is to first obtain the data records from each Web database (the process is called *Deep Web crawling* [Cafarella et al., 2011; Raghavan and Garcia-Molina, 2001] or *Surfacing*), put them into the same system and create a new Web database using the data. Another approach is to support unified access to multiple existing Web databases, usually from the same domain, without crawling their contents in advance. This is known as *metasearching*. Both methodologies require computer interactions with the query interfaces of individual Web databases. The latter further requires the integration of the query interfaces of multiple Web databases in the same domain. The goal of this book is to introduce representative techniques that have been developed to analyze and integrate the query interfaces of Web databases.

In this chapter, we provide some background and context for later chapters of the book. We will first take a closer look at the two main portions of the Web, namely, the *surface Web* and the *deep Web*. Then we will provide a brief overview of the key components of a typical deep Web search engine for structured data. Next we will provide more information about two main paradigms for enabling integrated access to multiple Web databases in the same domain, namely the Deep Web Crawling paradigm and the metasearching paradigm. The last section of this chapter will provide an overview of the rest of the book.

1.1   DEEP WEB VS. SURFACE WEB

The Web has long been recognized as consisting of two different segments – the *surface Web* and the *deep Web* (or *hidden Web*) [Bergman, 2001]. The former refers to the collection of Web pages that are publicly and directly accessible without the need to go through a registration, login, or the interface of a search engine. Usually, each such page has a static logical address called *Uniform Resource Locator* or URL. The latter contains Web contents that do not belong to the surface Web. Such Web contents include Web pages or documents that can be accessed only by paid users or by submitting queries to the query interfaces of some search systems. As an example, consider the case where a publisher has accumulated many articles in digital format, but these articles are not placed on the surface Web (i.e., there are no static URLs for them) and they are only accessible by Web users through the publisher's search engine. The articles in this example belong to the deep Web. The deep Web also contains Web-accessible structured data, such as data records, stored in database systems. Structured data are usually presented to the Web users as search result records in dynamically generated Web pages.

Web pages in the surface Web are mostly text documents in HTML format. These pages are usually linked to each other. As a result, it is easy to navigate from one page to another using a Web browser. The extensive linkage among these Web pages makes it possible to find a huge number of Web pages from a small number of seed Web pages. In contrast, most data in the deep Web are structured data records stored in backend database systems and there are usually no hyperlinks among these data records.

Due to the existence of extensive links among Web pages in the surface Web, it is possible to develop a computer program to fetch a huge number of Web pages starting from a set of well-connected seed Web pages. Such a program is called a *Web crawler* or a *Web spider*. A typical crawler takes the URLs of some seed Web pages as input to form an initial URL list. It then repeats the following two steps until either no new URLs can be found or enough pages have been fetched: (1) take the next URL from the URL list, establish connection to the server where the Web page resides, and fetch the corresponding Web page from its server by issuing an HTTP (HyperText Transfer Protocol) request to the server; (2) extract new URLs from each fetched Web page and add them to the list. In contrast, since the documents or data records in the deep Web are not hyperlinked like Web pages in the surface Web, the above link-based crawling technique cannot be used to fetch deep Web contents. Instead, a new technique known as *deep Web crawling* is needed to fetch contents from the deep Web. Deep Web crawling will be discussed in Section 1.3.1.

One important motivation for crawling Web contents from different hosting servers is to build search engines using the crawled data. All major existing search engines, such as Google, Bing and Yahoo!, are built using mainly Web pages crawled from the surface Web, although more and more Web contents crawled from the deep Web are being incorporated into some of these search engines such as Google [Cafarella et al., 2008; Madhavan et al., 2008, 2009]. The reason that most major search engines are focused on the data from the surface Web is because it is relatively easy to crawl a large portion of the surface Web using a Web crawler compared to crawling data from the deep Web. In comparison, because data in the deep Web are more isolated, which makes them difficult for large-scale crawling using today's deep Web crawling techniques, there still does not exist a search engine today that can search a large portion of the deep Web. As a result, search engines that exclusively search the deep Web are usually small and focus on the contents from one domain.

The exact size of the surface Web is unknown but the size of the indexed Web, which is the portion of the surface Web that is covered by major search engines, has been estimated to be around 50 billion Web pages recently (December 2011) according to http://www.worldwidewebsize. com/. The indexed Web is only a subset of the surface Web and no Web crawler is able to crawl the entire Web. According to a study of the graph structure of the Web [Broder et al., 2000], close to half of Web pages in the surface Web are not easily reachable by hyperlinks because these pages do not have backlinks. The exact size of the deep Web is also unknown and it is even more difficult to estimate. The "Deep Web Research 2012" report [Zillman, 2012] estimates that there are approximately

1 trillion pages of information in 2012. Although the exact sizes of the surface Web and the deep Web are both unknown, there is still a general consensus in the Web community that the deep Web is many times larger than the surface Web.

This book focuses on the query interface of search engines that search structured data in the deep Web.

1.2   WEB DATABASE TECHNOLOGY

Earlier, we defined a Web database as a search engine that searches structured data stored in backend database systems. In this section, we briefly review the main technologies for building a Web database. Figure 1.1 shows the main components of a typical Web database.

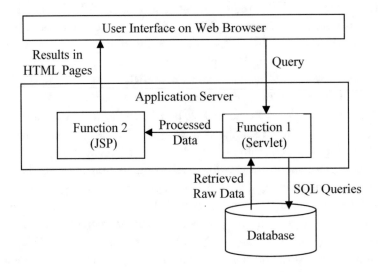

Figure 1.1: An architecture of Web Database.

We now discuss each of the components in more detail below.

User Interface. The function of user interface is for users to submit search queries and to view returned search results through a Web browser. For a Web database, the most important part of the user interface is a *query interface* that is used by users to enter search queries. A typical Web database query interface has multiple search fields for users to enter search conditions. Many of these search fields correspond to the attributes of the objects (e.g., products and services) the Web database is built to search. For example, the query interface of the book Web database AbeBooks.com[3] as shown in Figure 1.2 has four search fields and they correspond to four attributes of book records.

---

[3] Accessed on December 29, 2011.

Figure 1.2: The query interface of `AbeBooks.com`.

Query interfaces of Web databases are usually implemented using the HTML *form tag* (i.e., <form>...</form>), which is used to create HTML forms for accepting input from users. A typical HTML form of a Web database includes one or more *input controls*. Common types of input controls include textbox, selection list (i.e., pull-down menu), radio buttons, and checkboxes. For example, a textbox is implemented by <input type ="text" name ="name_string"/>, where the *name attribute* specifies the name of the input, and the search engine server uses it to identify the query string. The form also has an *action attribute* (e.g., action ="action_URL") that specifies the name and location of the Web database server to which the user query will be sent when the form is submitted and a *method attribute* (e.g., method ="post") that specifies the HTTP request method for sending the query to the Web database server. Other attributes and tags may also be included in a search form to specify additional features such as default settings, text styles, and the maximum length of the input text allowed. More complex forms may also include scripts, such as javascript. A good source for more complete discussion of the HTML form tag can be found at the W3 Web site (`http://www.w3.org/TR/html401/interact/forms.html`[4]). Figure 1.3 shows some of the key input controls and attributes of the form tag of the `AbeBooks.com` Web Database. It can be seen that this form has four text input controls.

After a user enters the search conditions and submits the query, the query will be sent to the Application Server by the browser as an HTTP request.

Application Server. The application server is a server side software that provides a context for program codes to be executed. Most application servers also have the functionalities of a Web server, which can receive HTTP requests and send HTTP responses. In most real world applications, web servers and application servers are used differently. Web servers are usually used to host static content such as static Web pages and images while application servers are widely used to host dynamic content such as dynamically generated Web pages whose main content comes from a database system.

---

[4]Accessed on December 29, 2011.

```
<form action="/servlet/SearchResults"
  method="post" name="homepageSearch"> ......
<td class="attributeHeader"
  align="right">Author:</td>
<input type="text" name="an"></td> ......
<td class="attributeHeader"
  align="right">Title:</td>
<input type="text" name="tn"></td> ......
<td class="attributeHeader"
  align="right">Keyword:</td>
<input type="text" name="kn"></td> ......
<td class="attributeHeader"
  align="right"> ISBN:</td>
<input type="text" name="isbn"></td> ......
<td class="button" align="left">
<input type="image"
  src="/images/Shared/findBook-large.gif"
  alt="FIND BOOK">
<a href="/servlet/SearchEntry" title="More
Search Options">More Search Options</a>
</td> </form>
```

Figure 1.3: An abbreviated HTML form of the query interface of the AbeBooks.com Web Database.

For a Web database, the application server has two main functions. The first function is for accepting the user queries sent from the browser, converting them to SQL queries, sending the SQL queries to the database system and processing the results returned from the database system. Servlets are commonly used to implement this function in Web applications. A servlet is a Java class in JEE (Java Enterprise Edition) that conforms to the Java Servlet API.

The second function is to generate the HTML output to be sent back to the browser for display to the user. It takes the processed results from the servlet and encodes them into presentation templates designed for the result pages. A widely used technology to achieve this is JSP (JavaServer Pages). JSP supports mixing Java code and HTML code. When the resulting page is compiled and executed, an HTML or XML document can be generated. JSP is also part of JEE.

JEE is currently one of the three main technologies for implementing Web application servers. The other two are PHP (PHP: Hypertext Preprocessor) and ASP (Active Server Pages).

Database System. The data records of the Web database are stored in a database system. The database system receives SQL queries from the application server and returns the retrieved results back to the application server. MySQL, Oracle, and Microsoft SQL Server have been widely used as backend database systems in Web databases.

For the rest of this subsection, we use a very simple example to further explain the main components of a Web database. In the example, we assume we have a table of products and each product has its name, price, and category. When users visit product-list.html?category = book, products belonging to the book category are retrieved from database, and a dynamic Web page containing a list of books is shown to the user. We use JEE technology and MySQL in this example. The following is a step-by-step explanation of the query evaluation process with the basic code snippets.

1. The user enters a query on the query interface of the Web database and submits it. The browser sends the query to the Application Server through an HTTP request.

2. The Application Server receives the request and selects a Servlet according to the request. A *method* in the Servlet is executed to handle the request. For example, if the request is an HTTP *get* request, the following doGet method is executed:

```
public class ProductListServlet extends
HttpServlet {
 @Override
 protected        void
doGet(HttpServletRequest req,
HttpServletResponse resp)
      throws ServletException, IOException {
      // Code to implement business logic
 }
}
```

The corresponding Servlet to use for each URL pattern is configured in the Application Server. Below is a sample configuration of a Servlet named ProductListServlet to handle request for URL /product-list.html.

```
<servlet>
  <servlet-name>
    ProductListServlet</servlet-name>
  <servletclass>
    com.sample.servlet.ProductListServlet
  </servlet-class>
</servlet>
<servlet-mapping>
  <servlet-name>ProductListServlet
  </servlet-name>
  <url-pattern>/product-list.html
  </url-pattern>
</servlet-mapping>
```

3. The Servlet reads information such as query parameters from the request, prepares the SQL query, obtains a connection to the database system, and sends the SQL query through the connection to the database system.

```
String category =
request.getParameter("category");
String sql = "SELECT * FROM products WHERE
category = '" + category + "'";
Connection conn = null;
Statement stmt = null;
ResultSet rs = null;
try {
    conn =
        DriverManager.getConnection("jdb
    c:mysql://localhost/shop" +
    "user=webUser&password=");
    stmt = conn.createStatement();
    rs = stmt.executeQuery(sql);
} catch (SQLException ex) {
    // handle any errors
}
```

In the above code snippet, Java Database Connectivity (JDBC) is used to access the database. It is an API for the Java programming language to access database. Connection, Statement, ResultSet, DriverManager are classes defined in the java.sql package, which is part of the JDBC API.

The string passed to the getConnection method is the *connection string*, which provides the information needed to connect to a database. It always starts with "jdbc:," followed by the name of the database type in use, which is "mysql" in the above example. Here "localhost" is the name of the database server, "shop" is the name of the database, username and password are encoded into the connection string as parameters.

In the above example code, a connection to the database is established through DriverManager, and then a Statement object is created to execute the SQL query and return the results that are wrapped in a ResultSet object rs, which is a table of data representing a database result set.

4. The database system receives the SQL query, executes it against the specified table(s), and returns the retrieved data back to the Servlet.

5. The Servlet receives the data, processes it as needed. Then the Servlet converts the data from ResultSet into Java objects:

```
List<Product> products = new
ArrayList<Product>();
while(rs.next()) {
        Product product = new Product();
 product.setName(rs.getString("NAME"));
        product.setPrice(rs.getDouble("PRICE")
);
        products.add(product);
}
```

6. The objects produced by the Servlet are put into the request, and then the control is forwarded to the corresponding JavaServer Pages:

```
request.setAttribute("products", products);
RequestDispatcher rd =
getServletContext().getRequestDispatcher("/
WEB-INF/product-list.jsp");
rd.forward(request, response);
```

7. The JSP outputs the data, and combines the data with the HTML code to produce an HTML output:

```
<%
List<Product> products = (List<Product>)
request.getAttribute("products");
for(Product p : products) {
%>
<h3><%= p.getName() %></h3>
<p><%= p.getPrice()%></p>
<% } %>
```

In the above code, contents within <% and %>are Java code and contents outside <% and %>are HTML code.

8. The Application Server sends the result from JavaServer Pages back to the browser for the user to view.

1.3   PARADIGMS FOR INTEGRATED ACCESS OF THE DEEP WEB

The structured data in the deep Web are scattered across a large number of Web databases. According to a 2007 study [Madhavan et al., 2007], there were already about 25 million searchable deep Web data sources (i.e., Web databases) on the Web. The proliferation of Web databases of such a scale causes several problems from the perspective of ordinary users. First, an ordinary user probably knows only a very small number of these Web databases. In other words, the user is likely unaware of most of these Web databases. If a user is not aware of a Web database, he/she certainly will not be able to use it. Second, even if a user is aware of a large portion of these Web databases, it will be very difficult for him/her to choose the right Web databases to use for his/her given information needs. Third, often a user needs to search multiple Web databases in order to find what he/she looks for. For example, the books the user needs may not all be available from the same book site or the user may need to search multiple book sites in order to find a good deal for a desired book. In these cases, it is inconvenient for the user to submit queries to multiple Web databases and examine multiple lists of results, even if the user knows which Web databases to use. One way to relieve these problems for ordinary users is to provide them with the capability to search the contents in all Web databases from a single query interface. We call this capability "integrated access" of the deep Web.

There are two general paradigms to enable integrated access of the deep Web. The first is *data collection* and the second is *metasearching*. In the data collection paradigm, data from deep Web sources are collected first, then a search index for the collected data is created, which is then used to provide the integrated access. In the metasearching paradigm, a search system with its own query interface is created and this search system can pass user queries to other Web databases and gather search results from them. Each of the two paradigms has its relative advantages and disadvantages. We review the two paradigms and their pros and cons in the following two subsections.

1.3.1   DATA COLLECTION

There are primarily two approaches to collect the structured data from the deep Web. The first can be called *data feed*, which is to let owners of structured data upload their data to the centralized search system. The second is called *deep Web crawling* or *deep Web surfacing*, which is to scoop up the data from Web databases through submitting queries to their query interfaces. The first approach has been used by major search engines as a way to get structured data, especially product data, from Web-based businesses. For example, Google Base[5] allows registered users to upload structured data. This approach can only collect a small fraction of the structured data from the deep Web. The second approach is more likely to reach a

---

[5]http://base.google.com/base/. Accessed on December 29, 2011.

larger portion of the deep Web and it has attracted much attention from both researchers and developers in the Web community [Barbosa and Freire, 2004; Jin et al., 2011; Madhavan et al., 2008; Raghavan and Garcia-Molina, 2001; Wu et al., 2006a]. For the rest of this subsection, we provide a brief review of the main challenges and techniques in the deep Web crawling approach.

To enable large-scale and automated deep Web crawling of structured data, several technical issues need to be solved. First, a method is needed to automatically discover the query interfaces of Web databases. Second, for each discovered Web database, its query interface needs to be automatically analyzed to figure out how to interact with the server of the Web database and how to formulate valid queries for the Web database. Third, a method is needed to automatically generate queries for each Web database to maximize the yield (i.e., retrieving the most data) with a small number of queries. Fourth, a method is needed to automatically extract the search result records embedded in the response pages returned by each Web database in response to queries. We briefly discuss each of the above issues below.

(a) *Automatic Web database query interface discovery.* While the contents of Web databases are in the deep Web, their query interfaces are in the surface Web. A three-step approach can be used to discover these query interfaces. First, employ a regular crawler to crawl Web pages of the surface Web. Second, check each crawled Web page to determine whether it contains a query interface. Note that almost all query interfaces of Web databases are implemented using the HTML form tag. Third, check each query interface to determine whether it is for searching structured data. If yes, then it is the query interface of a Web database.

The issue described in the second step has been investigated before [Cope et al., 2003; Wu et al., 2003]. The challenge is how to automatically differentiate *search forms* (query interfaces) from non-search forms. Examples of non-search forms include forms that are used for conducting a survey, sending an email, and Web account log-in (e.g., Web-based email account or bank account). One approach uses a decision tree classifier to differentiate search forms from non-search forms [Cope et al., 2003]. Another approach [Wu et al., 2003] classifies a form as a search form if the following two conditions are satisfied: (a) the form has a text input field and (b) at least one of a set of keywords such as "search," "query," or "find" appears either in the form tag or in the text immediately preceding or following the form tag.

One approach for the third step recognizes query interfaces with at least two input fields (one of them must be a text input) as query interfaces for structured data [Madhavan et al., 2007]. This is a rough estimate as many query interfaces for unstructured data also have multiple input fields. A more accurate solution is still needed.

(b) *Query interface analysis.* For the purpose of deep Web crawling, query interface analysis has three goals. The first goal is to extract Web database connection information, which typically consists of three types of information: (1) the name and location of the Web database server; (2) the HTTP request method (*get* or *post*) supported by the Web database; and (3) the name of each input control and its value if it exists. These three types of information can be found from the *action* attribute, the *method* attribute, and the *name* and *value* attributes of the input tag of the search form of the Web database, respectively. Additional information on how to deal with some special cases in extracting connection information and how to perform automatic search engine connection can be found in a recent book by Meng and Yu [2010].

The second goal of query interface analysis is to understand the meaning of each input field so that the appropriate type of query values can be used for the input field. This is especially important for text input fields because the valid values for other types of input such as selection list and radio buttons have been prespecified in the query interface. For example, for the *Author* field in Figure 1.2, only person names should be entered as search values. Attribute labels such as *Author* and *Title* in Figure 1.2 can be extracted by query interface extraction tools [Dragut et al., 2009c; He et al., 2007; Zhang et al., 2004]. The number of distinct field labels that can appear in the query interfaces in each application domain (e.g., book and car) is limited [He and Chang, 2003]. As a result, the type of appropriate values for each label can be manually specified.

The third goal of query interface analysis is to determine how to formulate valid queries. A query is called a *valid query* for a query interface if it is acceptable to the query interface regardless of whether any results are retrieved by the query. For example, if there is a required field on a query interface, then any query that does not provide a value for this field is invalid. The concept of *atomic query* can be used to characterize valid queries [Shu et al., 2007]. An atomic query is a minimum set of search fields whose values must be provided in order to form a valid query. A query interface may have multiple atomic queries. For example, each of the four search fields in Figure 1.2 forms an atomic query. An atomic query may also contain multiple search fields. For example, an atomic query in a flight reservation website for roundtrip must contain *Leaving_from*, *Going_to*, *Departing_Date* and *Returning_Date*. Atomic queries of a query interface can be identified by submitting probing queries to the query interface [Shu et al., 2007]. A query is valid if and only if it contains an atomic query. Knowing what queries are valid helps eliminate the possibility of generating invalid queries, which in turn can improve the productivity of deep Web crawling.

(c) *Automatic query generation*. A query interface of a Web database may have multiple input fields. If each input field has 1,000 different valid values, then the number of combination queries for a query interface with three input fields will be one billion. Thus, it is not practical to form all possible queries for each query interface for deep Web crawling. Furthermore, the number of possible values for text input fields, such as *Author* and *Title* in a book query interface, can far exceed 1,000. A common goal in deep Web crawling is to maximize the coverage of the contents of a Web database with a certain number of queries.

Wu et al. [2006a] introduced a method to select the best query values for a given text input field. In this method, each Web database is modeled as a distinct attribute-value graph, which transforms the crawling problem into a graph traversal problem that follows *relational links*. A relational link between two attribute values exists if they appear in the same record. Just like almost all existing deep Web crawling techniques, this method employs an iterative process to perform the crawling. It starts with some seed values, submits each of them to the query interface, obtains the retrieved results, selects new query values from the results and uses them for later iterations. When selecting the next query value to submit, this method basically favors those values that have more relational links to the records that have already been crawled. Furthermore, in later stages of the crawling, it penalizes query values that have strong dependency to already used query values in an effort to avoid query values that are likely to retrieve already retrieved records. This method also discussed how to leverage the domain knowledge (e.g., the distribution of attribute values among database records) derived from the already crawled Web database in the same domain to help select query values for crawling a new Web database in the same domain. One limitation of this method is that it considers only one input field in the query interface at a time but not combinations of input fields.

The method proposed by Madhavan et al. [2008] first identifies *informative query templates*, where a *query template* is a subset of the input fields in a query interface, and a query template is said to be *informative* if it can generate sufficiently different results for different input values to the input fields of the template. The method then identifies the appropriate values for each text input field following the widely used iterative probing technique. It starts with some seed words extracted from the query interface page, submits each seed word to the textbox, identifies new words from the retrieved results, clusters the new words such that words in the same cluster have similar content (e.g., synonyms), and selects one word from each cluster for the next iteration. It should be noted that the above method has a somewhat different goal from previous techniques (e.g., Wu et al., 2006b) in that it focuses less on exhaustively crawling the data from individual Web databases but more on achieving a good coverage from a large number of Web databases with a limited number of query submissions.

(d) *Automatic search result extraction*. Upon receiving a query, a typical Web database returns an initial response page with embedded database records retrieved from the backend database. Each response page has a link to the next response page, if it exists. Response pages are dynamically generated and they often also contain information that is not of interest to the deep Web crawler, such as advertisements. A portion of a response page from www.barnesandnoble.com is shown in Figure 1.4. In order to harvest such records automatically from a large number of Web databases, methods are needed to automatically extract them from the response pages and annotate them (assigning semantic labels to the data items in each record).

Figure 1.4: A portion of a response page from www.barnesandnoble.com (accessed on December 30, 2011).

Automatic search result record (SRR) extraction is a special case of Web information extraction. Two good surveys of Web information extraction techniques are Chang et al. [2006] and Laender and Ribeiro-Neto [2002]. Chapter 4 of Meng and Yu [2010] provides detailed review of several automatic SRR extraction techniques. These techniques include (1) those that use only HTML tag information (including DOM/tag tree) of the response pages, such as RoadRunner [Crescenzi et al., 2001], Omini [Buttler et al., 2001], DeLA [Wang and Lochovsky, 2003], and EXALG [Arasu and Garcia-Molina, 2003]; (2) those that also use visual information extracted from rendered response pages in addition to HTML tag information, such as ViNTs [Zhao et al., 2005], ViPER [Simon and Lausen, 2005], DEPTA [Zhai and Liu, 2006], and ViDRE [Liu et al., 2010]; and (3) those that also incorporate domain knowledge about the Web database under consideration, such as the method proposed by Embley et al. [1999] and the ODE system [Su et al., 2009]. A common methodology shared by most of these techniques is that during SRR extraction they try to identify the *query result section* on the input response page first and to extract the SRRs in the query result section using automatically determined SRR separator(s) afterward.

In order to restore the structure of the retrieved data from the deep Web, it is necessary to determine the semantic meaning of each data item in SRRs. For example, the first record in Figure 1.4 has several data items with semantic meanings such as title, publication time, author, publisher, etc. For most of these data items, their semantic meanings are not given in the response page. The issue of how to automatically assign semantic meanings to data items in retrieved SRRs has been studied in recent years [Lu et al., 2007, 2012; Su et al., 2009; Wang and Lochovsky, 2003; Zhu et al., 2006]. All of the methods require certain domain knowledge about the Web database under consideration. The method introduced by Wang and Lochovsky [2003] uses the information extracted from the query interface of the Web database as domain ontology while the method proposed by Su et al. [2009] additionally uses sample results retrieved from the Web database to enrich the ontology. The domain knowledge used by the method by Lu et al. [2007, 2012] includes the query interface of the Web database and the integrated query interface for the domain of the Web database[6]. The most recent method proposed by Lu et al. [2007, 2012] consists of two phases. The first phase is the *alignment* phase, in which data items in the SRRs are first identified and then organized into different groups with each group corresponding to a different concept (e.g., all titles are grouped together). The second phase is the *annotation* phase, which determines the semantic label for the data items within each group holistically. This annotation method consists of multiple basic annotators with each exploiting one type of feature and producing a label for each applicable group; then a probabilistic model is used to determine the final label for each group.

The advantages for the data collection paradigm includes: (1) the system will have possession of the collected data, which enables it to preprocess the data (e.g., linking the data collected from different sources and removing duplicates) as desired; (2) a search index can be created in advance to permit fast processing of user queries; and (3) the data collected from the deep Web can be searched together with the data collected from the surface Web uniformly, as Google has been doing in recent years [Cafarella et al., 2011; Madhavan et al., 2008]. On the other hand, this approach also has some serious limitations, including: (1) a large portion of the data in the deep Web cannot be crawled by the current deep Web crawling technology; and (2) it is extremely difficult to maintain the freshness of the crawled data because crawlers cannot keep up with the fast changing deep Web contents stored across a huge number of Web servers involved.

---

[6]Query interface integration will be covered in Chapter 6 of the book.

1.3.2   METASEARCHING

In the metasearching paradigm for providing integrated access to the deep Web, an integration system is built on top of different Web databases. Conceptually, this integration system works like a metasearch engine [Meng and Yu, 2010] or a federated search system [Shokouhi and Si, 2011]. It has its own query interface. Queries submitted to this interface are first translated to queries acceptable to the query interfaces of relevant Web databases and are then passed to these Web databases. When the integration system receives the results retrieved from individual Web databases, it integrates the results and displays the integrated results to the user. In reality, building such an integration system is quite challenging, mainly because Web databases are very diverse (i.e., they contain data with different structures) and are usually autonomous (i.e., each one is independently designed and operated). The vast differences among Web databases make it impossible to build a single integration system covering all of them. The current practice is to build a separate integration system for Web databases in each different domain. For example, one integration system can be built for all Web databases in the book domain and another for those in the car domain.

To build different integration systems over Web databases in different domains, we first need to discover all Web databases. This issue was briefly discussed in Section 1.3.1 earlier. Next, a method is needed to group the Web databases by their domains so that we can build an integration system for Web databases in each domain. This issue will be covered in detail in Chapter 3 of this book.

Most existing techniques for Web database clustering and categorization are based on utilizing the information available from the query interfaces of Web databases. These techniques require automatic extraction of information from Web database query interfaces that is useful for clustering and categorization. Query interface extraction is a very important issue as it is applicable to three components of building integration systems over Web databases: Web database connection (Section 1.3.1), Web database clustering and categorization (Chapter 3), and query interface integration (Chapters 4–6). In other words, in query interface extraction, we need to extract Web database connection information (Section 1.3.1), query interface content information for query interface clustering and classification, and query interface representation information (including content and structural information as well as metadata). Query interface extraction will be discussed in detail in Chapter 2.

To summarize, in this book, the entire process of creating an integrated query interface for each domain can be considered as consisting of five main steps as shown in Figure 1.5. In the first step, a query interface schema is extracted from the query interface HTML source of each Web database. In the second step, the extracted query interfaces are clustered by their domains. In the third step, matching attributes, namely attributes having similar semantics across different query interfaces in the same domain, are identified. In the fourth step, matched attributes across different query interfaces are integrated, including the integration of different features such as names, formats and external values of the matched attributes. In the fifth step, different query interfaces in the same domain are integrated. These five steps will be covered in detail in Chapters 2, 3, 4, 5, and 6, respectively.

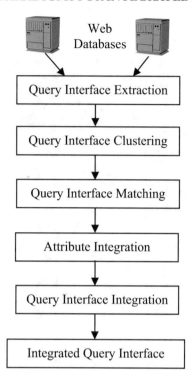

Figure 1.5: Query interface integration process.

In Figure 1.6, the main components of a typical Web database integration system are depicted. While they are also important on their own for building Web database integration systems, they are not the focus of this book. Therefore, we only summarize the basic ideas of these components here.

- *Database selection*. After a user query is received by the integrated query interface, this component determines which of the underlying Web databases should be used to process this current query [Kabra et al., 2005]. When the number of Web databases in an integration system is large, it is likely that many of them are not useful for a specific query. For example, for an integration system for the car domain, for a query that searches for a car of a particular make (e.g., GM) and a particular style (e.g., SUV), all Web databases that do not sell this type of cars should not be searched in order to avoid wasting unnecessary computing and network resources. To enable accurate database selection, information that characterizes the contents of each Web database needs to be collected in advance.

- *Query translation and dispatch*. This component is responsible for mapping each query submitted to the integrated query interface (such a query is called a *global query*) to a query or

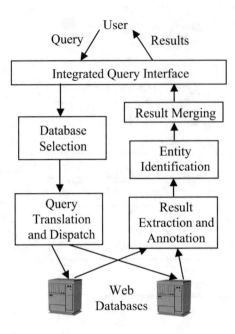

Figure 1.6: Architecture of a Web Database integration system.

queries, which are called *local queries*, against the local query interface of each of the selected Web databases. Query translation can be aided by a mapping table that maps each input field in the integrated query interface to the corresponding input field(s) in each local query inter-face. This mapping table has been constructed during query interface integration. Sometimes a global query interface may need to be translated to multiple queries against a local query interface. For example, this can happen when the price range, say [100, 200), in a global query corresponds to multiple price ranges, say [100, 150) and [150, 200), in a local query interface. It is also possible that some global queries cannot be translated to equivalent local queries for various reasons such as when a local query interface does not have a matching attribute used in a global query and when prespecified values of matching selection-list attributes do not match exactly (e.g., local price ranges covering [100, 200) are [50, 150) and [150, 250)). In this case, the global query is translated to a broader local query or queries to ensure the retrieval of all qualified results. At the same time, the integration applies post-processing to remove unqualified results. Query translation is not covered in this book but some related work can be found in the literature (e.g., Dhamankar et al., 2004; Zhang et al., 2005). Once a query against a local query interface is obtained, with the connection parameters for the corresponding Web database having already been extracted (see Section 1.3.1), passing the query to the server of the Web database is relatively straightforward (see Section 4.1 of the book by Meng and Yu [2010] for relevant technical details).

- *Result extraction and annotation.* This component is also needed for the deep Web crawling based paradigm and the basic ideas of this component has been discussed in Section 1.3.1.

- *Entity identification.* After the integration system receives the SRRs retrieved from different selected Web databases, its entity identification component is responsible for determining which SRRs from different sources actually correspond to the same real world entities. There are several reasons for performing entity identification. First, it allows the integration system to combine information about the same entity from multiple Web databases, which makes it possible to present more complete information about retrieved results to the user and/or identify qualified SRRs that cannot be determined by individual Web databases. For example, it is possible for a book record to be missing the publisher information in one source and to have incomplete author information in another source; by combining the information about the book retrieved from multiple sources, the integration system can provide more complete information about the book than individual sources. Second, it allows the integration system to highlight significant differences among the SRRs for the same entity that are retrieved from different sources. For example, in comparison-shopping applications, users are interested in the difference in prices for the same product. Third, it allows the integration system to identify and remove identical SRRs retrieved from different sources.

Entity identification is easy if the same unique identifier exists for the concerned entities across all sources, such as ISBN for books. Otherwise, attribute values of different SRRs need to be compared to determine whether two SRRs correspond to the same entity. Automatic entity identification across autonomous information sources has been a long standing challenging issue, and numerous solutions have been proposed to tackle this problem [Elmagarmid et al., 2007]. The basic methodology for determining whether two SRRs correspond to the same entity consists of two steps. In the first step, a matching score is computed between the values under the same attribute for each attribute of the two SRRs. For example, to compute the matching scores between two values of character strings, different variations of edit-distance function can be used [Elmagarmid et al., 2007]. In the second step, the matching scores for different attribute value pairs of the SRRs are used to determine whether the two SRRs are matched. Solutions for this step include Bayes network, machine learning, clustering, and rule-based techniques [Elmagarmid et al., 2007].

- *Result merging.* This component is for combining the results returned from different Web databases and presenting the merged results to users in certain desirable ways. For example, the integration system may compute a ranking score for each (possibly merged) result and display the results to the user in descending order of the ranking scores, as being done in many top-k systems [Ilyas et al., 2008]. In comparison-shopping applications, products can be first ranked in descending order of their lowest price from different sources.

By directly passing user queries to individual Web databases to search for results, the metasearching paradigm yields several benefits for the users over the data collection paradigm. First, the problem of not being able to crawl all the contents from deep Web sources suffered by the data collection approach simply disappears because the metasearching approach can effectively access the full contents of each Web database used in the integration system. Second, no crawling delay exists, which means that the users of the integration system can always have access to the most up-to-date information in Web databases, eliminating another serious problem of the data collection based approach. Third, this approach maximally takes advantage of the storage and computing resources already invested in operating Web databases, which means that it would cost less to run Web database integration systems. In addition, this approach provides a more natural way to access the deep Web sources, i.e., search what users need from the query interfaces of Web databases, just like how each individual Web database is designed to be used. Nevertheless, this approach also has its problems. First, by gathering data (i.e., query results) through autonomous Web databases on the fly and by performing many tasks (i.e., database selection, query translation, result extraction and annotation, entity identification, and result merging) also on the fly, users may not get the results from the integration system as quickly as from a regular search engines. Second, many deep Web sources may not have clear domains [Madhavan et al., 2007], which makes it difficult to classify them into specific domains. Third, with this approach, it is impossible to link the deep Web data with other types of data in advance, limiting the usage of the data in some applications. Fourth, when individual Web databases change, the integration system needs to make appropriate adjustments in order to operate properly. For example, if the results from a Web database are displayed using a different pattern, the result extraction subsystem of the integration system needs to be modified.

1.4   BOOK OVERVIEW

The rest of the book will focus on different aspects of working with the query interfaces of Web databases, including extraction, clustering, and integration. We now provide a brief overview of each of the remaining chapters.

In Chapter 2, we first provide a thorough analysis of some common features and properties of deep Web query interfaces. Then we present two widely used query interface representation models, one treating all attributes at the same level and the other organizing the interface schema into a hierarchical structure. We also review a number of query interface extraction techniques, some of which are based on analyzing the HTML source code of the form tag of the query interfaces, some of which utilize visual information available on rendered query interface on a browser to perform extraction, and some of which use both tag information and visual information for query interface extraction.

In Chapter 3, we cover three issues. The first is how to discover Web databases. The second is how to perform query interface clustering. The third is how to categorize query interfaces into different domains.

In Chapter 4, we focus on issues related to attribute matching. We first briefly review techniques for matching attributes across traditional database schemas. We then analyze the differences between attribute matching across different database schemas and attribute matching across different query interfaces. From this analysis, we identify new challenges in matching attributes across query interfaces. Finally, we introduce different types of attribute matching techniques for query interfaces, including clustering based techniques, statistical based techniques and instance based techniques.

In Chapter 5, we introduce techniques for integrating matched attributes. We start with reviewing some basic attribute integration methods involving traditional database schemas. We then describe several attribute integration issues that are more specific to query interfaces. These issues include selecting the names and domain types of global attributes and integrating the values of matched attributes.

In Chapter 6, we take on the task of query interface integration based on the assumption that attribute-level matching and integration has been performed. We first review some basic techniques for traditional database schema integration. We then discuss issues related to integrating query interfaces. The last part of this chapter provides some discussion on issues related to naming/labeling integrated query interfaces in the context of the hierarchical interface representation model.

In Chapter 7, we summarize the main discussions of this book, discuss future directions for query interface integration, and introduce some remaining research challenges.

CHAPTER 2

Query Interface Representation and Extraction

Automatic interaction with Web databases hinges upon a thorough understanding of their query interfaces. Query interface understanding is the process of extracting semantic information from query interfaces. A query interface contains an (ordered) set of interface components: *text-labels* and *form elements* (textbox, selection list, etc.). Most query interfaces are represented in HTML, lack a formal specification, and are developed independently. In addition, semantically related elements on a query interface are scattered in HTML text and the formal associations of these elements do not exist, or are very limited. HTML is a markup language, designed for formatting web pages but not for expressing data structures and semantics. HTML has a rather loose grammar and browsers often do not rigorously enforce the grammar when displaying HTML pages. As a result, ill-written HTML pages can often still be displayed by browsers and used by people. Query interface design seems rather heuristic in nature: there is no clear guidance of how to create such an interface. Query interfaces often follow different design patterns. For example, the orientation of labels can vary; it can vary both within a query interface as well as across query interfaces. For example, some *fields* in Figure 2.1 have the *labels* (labels are also called *field names* or simply *names*) above (e.g., "From") and some have them on the right (e.g., "Adults"). In addition, query interfaces that look similar can be developed with different HTML constructs. Therefore, while users can understand query interfaces with relative ease, machine processing of these interfaces is very challenging. Search fields on query interfaces are implemented as input control elements such as textboxes and selection lists. In this book, we use *fields* and (input) *elements* interchangeably.

Query interface extraction is a two-step process: (1) *modelling* and (2) *processing*. In the modelling step, a model is developed for query interfaces. In the processing step, an algorithm is developed to map a query interface to a representation consistent with the model used. Models for representing interfaces range from a simple enlisting of fields with their associated labels [Kaljuvee et al., 2001; Nguyen et al., 2008] to a hierarchical structure where fields are grouped based on their semantic roles on the interface [Dragut et al., 2009c; He et al., 2007; Wu et al., 2009]. A number of query interface extraction algorithms have been developed [Khare et al., 2010]. They can be classified along several dimensions:

1. the underlying models used for representing query interfaces,

2. the input data (e.g., HTML source code versus visual rendering) or

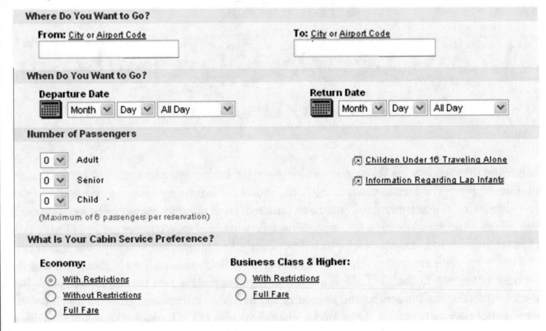

Figure 2.1: Example of a query interface in the airfare domain.

3. the underlying paradigms employed by the extraction algorithms (e.g., visual grammars [Zhang et al., 2004], learning classifiers [Nguyen et al., 2008], hierarchical agglomerative spatial clustering [Wu et al., 2009]).

In this chapter we first present a comprehensive model for representing query interfaces, then we describe some alternative models and present several extraction algorithms. For each algorithm we mention the underlying query interface model, the input data, and the key characteristics.

2.1   CHARACTERISTICS OF DEEP WEB QUERY INTERFACES

The basic building blocks of query interfaces are *text input boxes*, *selection lists*, *radio buttons*, and *check boxes*. We will generically call them *elements* or *fields*. A text input box is rendered as an empty box with or without a default value. The element "From" in the interface in Figure 2.1 is such an element. A selection list presents the user with a set of choices to select from. There are two types of selection lists: *single selection list* (e.g., combo box) and *multiple selection list* (e.g., listbox). Radio buttons and check boxes are employed by designers to explicitly display the choices to the user. For example, in Figure 2.1 the "Economy" *attribute* is shown as a set of radio buttons. The difference between radio buttons and check boxes is that choices are exclusive in a radio button group, whereas multiple check boxes may be selected at the same time. A radio button group can be regarded as a single selection list and a group of check boxes as a multiple selection list. For example, the set of radio buttons denoting the economy class is treated as an element (single selection list) whose label is "Economy." Labels attached to individual radio buttons (e.g., "With Restrictions") become the *values* of the selection list. The same applies to the labels attached to checkboxes. To summarize, we have two types of fields in query interfaces: fields with predefined values and fields without predefined values.

Each field has an *internal name*, which identifies the field in the HTML source (for programming purposes). A field may have a *label* that describes to users the meaning of the field. Some fields may not have their own labels; rather they may share a label with a group of fields. For instance, the three fields denoting the departure date in Figure 2.1 do not have their own labels, but they share a *group label*. In some cases the label may be entirely left out as the designer relies on the set of values of the field to convey the semantics of the field. While internal names are readily available from HTML source of a query interface page, the assignment of labels requires substantial work, but is necessary for the correct understanding of the semantics of a field or a group of fields. Logically, certain fields and their associated labels together form an *attribute* (or query condition) of the underlying database.

When an attribute has multiple associated fields, they are classified into two types: *domain fields* and *constraint fields*, because they usually play different roles in specifying a query. Domain fields are used to specify domain values for the attribute, while constraint fields specify some constraints on domain fields. For example, in Figure 2.2, element "Exact phrase" is a constraint field, whereas the textbox following "Title keywords" is a domain field. Each attribute has a *name*. If an attribute has just one domain field, the name of the attribute is usually (not always) the label of this field. If an attribute has multiple domain fields, a separate name is often defined for the attribute. In Figure 2.2, attribute "Publication Year" has two domain fields (two textboxes with their own labels "after" and "before") and it has its own name (i.e., "Publication Year") which is not a label of any field.

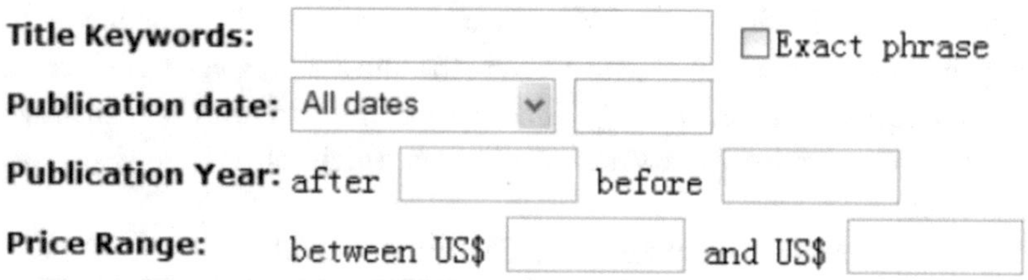

Title Keywords:	☐ Exact phrase
Publication date: All dates	
Publication Year: after before	
Price Range: between US\$ and US\$	

Figure 2.2: Example of an interface in the book domain.

In this book, the term *label* may have four different meanings depending on the context of its usage. It can be a *value* when it is the label of a radio button or checkbox, a *name* of a field when it is the label of a textbox or a selection list, a *name* of an attribute (see the above discussion), or even a name of a group of fields/attributes. As an example for using a label as a name of a group, in Figure 2.1, "Where Do You Want to Go?" is the label or name of a group of two attributes "From" and "To." In this book, we use label and name interchangeably when the label is not referring to a value.

2.1.1   QUERY INTERFACE METADATA

Mature data models (e.g., relational model) have well-defined formalisms (e.g., normal forms) to systematically judge when a database schema is or is not well-designed. Analogously, we need to lay down a set of properties that facilitates a precise characterization of a query interface. This allows the development of algorithms for manipulating query interfaces with desirable properties, e.g., query interface extraction and integration algorithms. In this section, we present a schema model for Web query interfaces that captures rich semantic information [Dragut et al., 2009c; He et al., 2007]. A query interface is represented by the triple $F = (S, A, C_f)$, where S is the site information associated with the query form (e.g., the site URL, the server name and the HTTP request method), $A = \langle A_1, A_2, ..., A_n \rangle$ is an ordered list of attributes on the interface, and C_f is the form constraint (the logic relationship of the attributes for query submission). Each A_i is represented as $(L, DT, DF, VT, U, R_e, E, C_a)$, where L is the *label* (*name*) of A_i (if applicable), DT is the *domain type* of A_i (e.g., textbox and selection list), DF is the *default value* of A_i, VT is the *value type* of A_i (e.g., number, date and char), U is the unit of A_i (e.g., unit of length or weight), $E = \langle E_j, E_{j+1}, ..., E_k \rangle$ is an ordered list of *domain fields* of A_i, R_e is the *relationship type* of the domain fields, and C_a is the constraints of the attribute. For fields of textbox domain type, it is difficult to determine what kind of input the field expects in general [Jin et al., 2011; Madhavan et al., 2008; Wu et al., 2006b]. The default value of a textbox can be a valuable indicator of the kind of input such a field expects [Cafarella et al., 2008]. Each domain field E_i is itself represented as (L_e, N, F_e, V, DV), where L_e is the *field label* (possibly empty), N is the *internal name* of the field, F_e is the *format* (e.g., textbox, selection list, checkbox and radio button), V is the set of *values* of E_j in the query interface (e.g., the choices of a selection list), and DV is the *default value* of E_j (possibly null). The set of attributes A as well as the set of fields E within each attribute are organized in a tree data structure. We describe the tree structure in Section 2.2.2. The order of the attributes in A and that of the fields in each E is given by the depth-first traversal of the tree, which reflects the visual ordering of the fields on the interface.

Both A and E are ordered sets of elements. Changing the order of the fields in E may change the semantics. For example, changing the order of the fields of "From" and "To" in Figure 2.1 would make the semantics of the interface very confusing. Changing the order of the attributes in A would not necessarily affect the semantics of attributes, but it may affect the semantics or the understanding of the query interface. For example, the interface in Figure 2.1 would be very confusing for a user if the attribute "Return Date" were moved ahead of "Departure Date." The order reflects the importance as well as how the grouping of the attributes on the query interface is perceived by the designers or users.

We explain some of the concepts in the interface schema model next, while the rest of the concepts are explained in subsequent sections.

Relationships Among Fields

An attribute may have multiple fields and the fields may be related differently within an attribute. Generally, there exist four types of field relationships: *range type*, *part type*, *group type*, and *constraint type*. For example, in Figure 2.2, the relationship between the fields of the attribute "Publication Year" is of range type (for specifying range query conditions); the relationship of the fields of "Departure Date" in Figure 2.1 is of part type (i.e., *month*, *day*, and *time* are all parts of a *date*); the relationship formed by the radio buttons of "Economy" is of group type; and finally "Exact phrase" is a constraint type as it specifies a constraint on "Title keywords."

Identifying the relationship between the fields of each attribute helps interface schema integration and query mapping. As an example for query mapping, consider a local query interface containing an attribute "Title keywords" as shown in Figure 2.2. When a user specifies a query on the global attribute "Title" in an integrated interface, the query translator should map the query value to the domain field of "Title keywords" instead of the constraint field "Exact phrase."

Field Label

In Figure 2.2, the attribute "Publication Year" has two fields whose labels are "after" and "before," respectively. In this case, "Publication Year" is treated as the label of the attribute. Field labels are considered the child labels of their attribute, which usually represent the semantics of the fields.

Logic Relationship of Attributes

Attributes on a query interface can be logically combined in different ways to form a query to access the underlying database. Correctly identifying the logic relationship is important for successful query mapping and submission. Generally, there are four possibilities:

1. *Conjunctive.* All the attributes are combined through the "and" Boolean logic operator, meaning that all specified conditions must be satisfied at the same time.

2. *Disjunctive.* All the attributes are combined through the "or" Boolean logic operator, meaning that at least one of the specified conditions must be satisfied.

3. *Exclusive.* In this case, only one attribute can be chosen to form a query at any given time. In Figure 2.3, the attribute names appear as a group of radio buttons and only one attribute can be used at a time to form a query.

4. *Hybrid.* This is a combination of two or more of the above three cases. In this hybrid case, some conditions may be conjunctive, some may be disjunctive, and some may be exclusive [He et al., 2007].

Example 2.1 The attribute "Price Range" on the query interface in Figure 2.2 can be represented as (Price Range, 4, range, null, currency, USD, range, {("Between US$," "low," textbox, Ø, null),

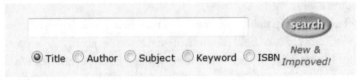

Figure 2.3: Query interface of BestBookBuys.

("And US$," "high," textbox, Ø, null)}, Ø), where "low" and "high" are the internal names of the two textboxes in the HTML text, and Ø denotes an empty set of constraints.

2.1.2   DOMAIN SPECIFIC PROPERTIES OF QUERY INTERFACES

Each Web database usually provides access to data in a certain domain such as auto, books, hotels, etc. Query interfaces of the Web databases from the same domain usually share similar characteristics. Studies about the properties of the query interfaces in some domains have been reported.

The survey reported in Chang et al. [2004] studied 441 query interfaces in eight different domains. These domains and the numbers of Web databases in them are Airfares (50), Automobiles (97), Books (59), Car Rentals (24), Hotels (39), Jobs (52), Movies (69), and Music Records (51). One property they studied is the size of query interface schema, i.e., the number of attributes in a query interface. The average number of attributes for query interfaces among the eight domains range from about five (Movies and Music Records) to about nine (Airfares and Car Rentals). The smallest query interface just has one attribute (a Movies query interface) while the largest one has 18 attributes (a Books query interface). These findings show that the sizes of query interface schemas vary significantly among different interfaces either within the same domain or across different domains.

This survey also made four interesting observations about the attribute labels (names) in the query interfaces in different domains. First, there is a *clustering behavior* among the attributes, i.e., certain attributes have high co-occurrence correlations (e.g., *Author* and *Title*). Second, the *convergence behavior* can be observed, i.e., the vocabulary of the attribute labels of the query interfaces in the same domain tends to converge at a relatively small size. Third, the frequencies of attributes, i.e., the numbers of query interfaces attributes appearing in them follow a clear Zipf-like distribution, i.e., the frequencies of attributes are inversely proportional to the ranks of the attributes in descending order of the frequency. Fourth, there is a *linking behavior* among the attributes in query interfaces from different domains, i.e., semantic-relatedness of different domains are often reflected by the amount of common attributes among the query interfaces of the domains – having more attributes in common indicates higher semantic-relatedness.

In a different study [Dragut et al., 2009b], after analyzing the content words (735 in total) from 2,319 labels in 9 distinct domains, it was found that within each application domain the occurrence of words with multiple meanings (i.e., homonyms) is extremely rare. Only one of the 735 distinct content words has multiple senses. This is the word "area" in the Real Estate domain and it has distinct senses in the labels "Minimum floor area" and "Select an area" (the latter refers to a location).

2.2   QUERY INTERFACE REPRESENTATION MODELS

This section presents an overview of the query interface representation models. We broadly classify them into two categories: *flat* and *hierarchical*. The main difference between the two classes is that the former models view query interfaces as a simple list of fields with labels, while the latter models attempt to provide additional understanding, such as of the role of the fields (i.e., whether a field is a query value or a query condition), the relationship among fields (e.g., multiple input elements may form a semantic unit of information; for instance, "Adult," "Senior," and "Child" in Figure 2.1 form the semantic unit "Number of Passengers") and the order of the fields on a query interface. Query interface modelling is not the task of capturing the information needed to reproduce an interface in the way a human perceives it, but the task of collecting as rich a set of information as possible so that applications that rely on query interfaces for exploring the deep Web can be successfully accomplished. For example, data analytics applications over Web databases (e.g., estimating the database size) post queries to databases to draw statistics that allow third-parties to infer valuable aggregate information about the databases: e.g., quality, freshness, and content bias. These applications rely on good understanding of query interfaces for posting the right queries to the underlying hidden databases.

2.2.1   FLAT REPRESENTATION

Early works on understanding query interfaces assume that query interfaces are flat, i.e., containing a set of fields. Their focus is largely on extracting the fields with their corresponding data values, if available, and attaching the right labels to the fields on the interface. Abstractly, a flat representation of a query interface F is given by $F = (S, E)$, where $E = \{E_1, E_2, ..., E_n\}$ is a set of n fields, S is the site information associated with the form [Nguyen et al., 2008; Raghavan and Garcia-Molina, 2001; Shestakov et al., 2005]. A field can be any one of the standard input elements. Each field E_i has additional information such as the field label, its internal name, F_e – the set of values, and its default value (possibly null).

2.2.2   HIERARCHICAL REPRESENTATION

Hierarchical representations of query interfaces regard an interface as structured objects organized hierarchically [Dragut et al., 2009c; Wu et al., 2009]. An important aspect of query interfaces is a sort of spatial locality property among the fields. That is, semantically related fields are usually grouped together in an interface. For example, in the query interface in Figure 2.1, the fields denoting the types of passengers travelling are next to each other. Moreover, several related fields can further be grouped together. In the interface in Figure 2.1, the two groups of fields denoting departure date and return date, respectively, are put together under "When Do You Want to Go?" Thus, this bottom-up characterization gives rise to a hierarchical structure for interfaces. In addition, each group of fields may have labels that describe to the user what the group is about.

The proposed hierarchical models are of two types: *two levels* [He et al., 2007; Khare and An, 2009; Zhang et al., 2004] and *arbitrary number of levels* [Dragut et al., 2009c; Wu et al., 2009].

Two-Level Hierarchies

The two-level hierarchies arise from modelling a query interface as an ordered list of triplets of the form [attribute name, operator(s), operand(s)]. The triplets are called *query condition patterns* [Zhang et al., 2004]. For example, ["Title Keywords," "Exact Phrase," text] is a condition pattern in the query interface in Figure 2.2. Users can then use the condition to formulate a specific constraint, for example, "Title Keywords = "JohnSmith" by selecting an operator (e.g., "Exact Phrase") and filling in a value (e.g., "John Smith"). This model is further generalized by He et al. [2007]. These models along with the ones by Furche et al. [2011] and Khare and An [2009] are particular cases of the schema tree model, which we introduce next.

Arbitrary-Depth Hierarchies

The hierarchical structure of query interfaces was first hypothesized by Wu et al. [2004]. A query interface is an ordered tree of elements so that leaves correspond to the fields in a query interface, internal nodes correspond to groups of fields in the interface, and the order among the sibling nodes within the tree resemble the order of fields in the interface (from left-to-right). This schema tree captures both the order semantics and the nested grouping of the fields in a query interface. Figure 2.4 shows the corresponding schema tree of the query interface in Figure 2.1.

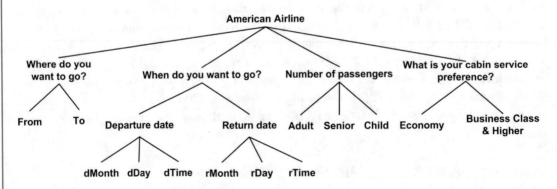

Figure 2.4: Schema tree of the query interface in Figure 2.1.

Observe that the schema tree in Figure 2.4 has four levels and that each level except the root refines the information in the level above. The first level is a generic root node (usually the root has the name of the website). Other types of meta-information can be attached to the leaves (fields) and internal nodes (groups of fields): domain type, default value, logic relationship, etc.

Motivation for Hierarchical Representation

We provide concrete examples of applications that utilize query interfaces and show how these applications would benefit from a hierarchical representation of query interfaces.

> **Query Interface Matching.** Matching of fields across a set of query interfaces can be significantly improved when interfaces are represented hierarchically. Among others, hierarchical representation helps avoid false matches due to the *homonymy problem* and to identify complex matchings (e.g., is-a and part-of relationships). An example of the former is provided by the label "From" in Figure 2.5 (left half) which is used to denote both *year* and *price* (right half). Unless the labels of the internal nodes are considered, when matching the interfaces in Figure 2.5, false matches may be derived, such as Year.From = Price.From.

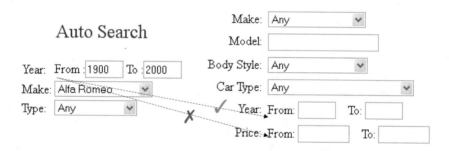

Figure 2.5: Example of homonym problem.

> **Deep Web Crawling.** The Deep Web crawling [Bergholz and Chidlovskii, 2003; Fang et al., 2007; Madhavan et al., 2008; Raghavan and Garcia-Molina, 2001; Wang et al., 2004; Wu et al., 2006a; Zhang et al., 2011] requires the understanding of query interfaces. A crawler needs to input meaningful values into the fields of query interfaces to retrieve the data from Web databases. It is observed that a preorder traversal of the schema tree of a query interface reflects the way a human being parses the interface in order to understand the meaning of the fields. This corresponds to "from top to bottom" and "from left to right" parsing of the query interface (or a document in general in the Western world) by a human user. For instance, in Figure 2.1, before a user reaches the field "From," the user first encounters the label "Where Do You Want to Go?" Thus, the user has an unambiguous understanding of the meaning of the field "From." A proper annotation of the nodes of the schema tree of a query interface could help a crawler automatically understand the meaning of the fields within the interface. The crawler can follow the same preorder traversal that a human uses to parse the interface.

Inter-related Fields. Another challenge to automatic understanding of query interfaces is the presence of inter-related fields. These fields restrict the kind of queries that can be submitted to a Web database. For example, in the query interface on the left-hand side of Figure 2.5, the fields Make and Type are related. The selection of a value in the field Make restricts the possible values shown in the field Type. The problem faced by a crawler is to determine those related fields from the Cartesian product of fields. The search space can be significantly reduced as such fields are siblings in the hierarchical representation.

2.3   QUERY INTERFACE EXTRACTION

Query interface extraction is the (automatic) process of mapping a query interface from its representation in a Web page to a workable physical structure. The workable physical structure is represented according to a query interface model (e.g., the hierarchical model). The input to a query interface extraction tool consists of the HTML source code of a query interface and/or its visual counterpart, i.e., the interface as viewed on a Web browser. An extraction tool has two main components: a *parsing component* and a *logic component*. All extraction tools have at least an HTML parser component. The pieces of information sought by the parser are of two kinds: (1) the elements displayed on the interface, and (2) the HTML elements and attributes (e.g., tags) that shape the layout of a query interface. The former category includes the input HTML elements (fields), their labels, their types (e.g., radio button, textbox) and the pieces of text shown on the interface. The latter category of information includes the HTML tags that may hold clues to understanding the relationships between the elements on an interface. For example, HTML tags such "
," "<P>," or "</TR>" may be used to determine which fields and texts appear in the same row in a query interface [He et al., 2007]. Styling information (e.g., font style and typefaces) may provide valuable insight into understanding query interfaces and is extracted from the HTML code as well [Dragut et al., 2009c; Furche et al., 2011]. Additionally, visual rendering of query interfaces on Web browsers can further enhance our ability to accurately map query interfaces to a representation model [Dragut et al., 2009c; Furche et al., 2011; Zhang et al., 2004]. For instance, the placement of the HTML elements for "Departure date" and "Return date" in a row in Figure 2.1 suggests that they form a (larger) semantic unit called "When Do You Want to Go?" Most extraction techniques, however, ignore styling and visual information in query interfaces [He et al., 2007; Kaljuvee et al., 2001; Khare and An, 2009; Nguyen et al., 2008; Raghavan and Garcia-Molina, 2001; Shestakov et al., 2005].

The logic component uses the information gathered by the parsing component about a query interface to map the interface to the desired representation model. This component should accomplish four tasks in general. (1) *Text-label assignment* is the task of associating an HTML form element with the appropriate surrounding text-label, e.g., the text "Adult" must be associated with the selection list to its left in Figure 2.1. (2) *Grouping* is the task of putting the fields into semantically related sets. For instance, the fields of "Departure Date" are an example of such a group in Figure 2.1. (3) *Semantic labeling* is the task of tagging fields and groups of fields with their semantic roles. For instance, He et al. [2007] assign the semantic labels "attribute-label," "domain/constraint element," and "element label" to the elements in a query interface. (4) *Meta-information annotation* is the task of tagging fields and groups with additional information, such as data type and unit of measurements. Carrying out these tasks automatically is challenging. For instance, automatic text label assignment and grouping are difficult due to diversity in Web design. The automatic detection of the label of an element is difficult because Web designers usually do not assign explicit labels to elements in the HTML source code.

The majority of extraction tools, e.g., LITE [Raghavan and Garcia-Molina, 2001], Comb-Match [Kaljuvee et al., 2001], DEQUE [Shestakov et al., 2005], and LabelEx [Nguyen et al., 2008], only address the text-label assignment task. Several extraction tools, however, go beyond this task. WISE-*i*Extractor [He et al., 2007] groups related text-labels and fields together into logical attributes. It also identifies the *exclusive attributes* in a query interface based on a domain-specific vocabulary. HSP [Zhang et al., 2004] finds groups of query condition patterns. WISE-*i*Extractor, HSP, and HMME [Khare and An, 2009] perform some grouping as well as semantic labeling. The representation models of these tools are instances of the two-level hierarchy model. VisQIExt [Dragut et al., 2009c] performs text-label assignment and creates groups and subgroups resulting into a tree of interface tokens. ExQ [Wu et al., 2009] extracts the grouping information of a query interface into an unlabeled tree structure and then performs text-label assignment to generate a labeled tree.

2.3.1 HEURISTIC-BASED EXTRACTION

The heuristics are of three kinds: textual, styling and layout. Textual heuristics include mainly string similarity measures between labels and internal names of fields. Below is an example of a heuristic [He et al., 2007; Kaljuvee et al., 2001]:

The label and the internal name of the same field may have some words/characters in common.

In the example of Figure 2.1, the internal name of the field *Adult* is "numAdult" and its label is "Adult." Since "numAdult" and "Adult" share a significant portion of text, their similarity score is high enough to suggest that the latter is the label of the field.

Styling heuristics include font size, font type, form element format, etc. Layout properties include position of a component, distance between two components, etc. LITE [Raghavan and Garcia-Molina, 2001], CombMatch [Kaljuvee et al., 2001], and WISE-*i*Extractor [He et al., 2007] exploit all three kinds of heuristics to perform text-label assignment. DEQUE [Shestakov et al., 2005] performs text-label assignment based on the textual and layout properties of components. WISE-*i*Extractor is a good representative of the heuristic-based extraction tools, because it performs well across many domains and is often used as a benchmark. WISE-*i*Extractor is part of the WISE Web database integration system [He et al., 2005]. The algorithm of WISE-*i*Extractor is introduced below.

WISE-*i*Extractor consists of two main components: one is attribute extraction which extracts logical attributes from query interfaces and identifies an appropriate label (name) for each attribute, and the other is attribute analysis which extracts a variety of meta-information about each attribute. WISE-*i* Extractor's attribute extraction algorithm consists of the following three steps.

1. *Generate Interface Expression.* WISE-*i* Extractor hypothesizes that labels and fields on a query interface are visually arranged in one or more rows by a browser. It captures the visual layout of labels and fields using the concept of *interface expression* (IEXP). For a given query interface, its IEXP is a string consisting of three types of items: 't', 'e', and '|', where 't' denotes a text, 'e' denotes a field, and '|' denotes a row delimiter, which represents a physical row border on the query interface. For example, the interface expression of the query interface in Figure 2.6 is "te|eee|te|eee|te|eee|te|te," where the first 't' denotes the label "Author," the first 'e' denotes the textbox following the label "Author," the first '|' denotes starting the second row as shown in Figure 2.6, and the following three 'e's denote the three radio buttons below the textbox (the text on a radio button/checkbox is treated as the value of the element in this approach, thus the text and its radio button/checkbox together are considered a whole entity). The remaining 't's, 'e's, and '|'s can be understood in a similar manner. '|' is appended to the IEXP when a row delimiter like "
," "<P>," or "</TR>" is encountered. The IEXP provides a high-level description of the visual layout of different labels and HTML elements.

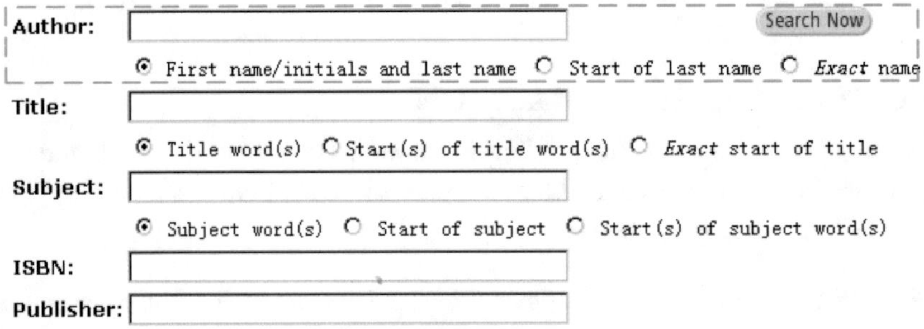

Figure 2.6: Example of another interface in the book domain.

2. *Identify the Labels of Exclusive Attributes.* The labels of exclusive attributes usually appear as *values* in some fields such as a group of *radio buttons* (e.g., Figure 2.3) or a *selection list*. Exclusive attributes appear frequently on real query interfaces (about 34% of the interfaces in books, movies, and music domains have exclusive attributes [He et al., 2007]). It can be observed that for a given domain the labels of exclusive attributes are often the *most commonly used attribute labels* of a domain. By considering many query interfaces in the same domain at the same time during interface extraction, a vocabulary of the common attribute labels for the domain can be extracted from the query interfaces. These labels have relatively high *interface frequencies* (i.e., they appear in many query interfaces in the same domain). For example, for the book domain, the vocabulary likely contains labels such as title, author, ISBN, etc. When determining whether a set of values associated with a set of radio buttons or a selection list in

a query interface of a certain domain is in fact a set of labels of exclusive attribute, the set of values is checked against the label vocabulary of the domain. If a high percentage of the values appears in the vocabulary, these values are recognized as the labels of exclusive attributes. For example, the values associated with the radio buttons in Figure 2.3 are {title, author, subject, keyword, ISBN}; since most of them, if not all, are frequent attribute labels in the book domain, they can be recognized as labels of exclusive attributes in the query interface in Figure 2.3.

3. *Group Labels and Fields into Logical Attributes.* WISE-*i* Extractor attempts to group the labels and elements that semantically correspond to the same logical attribute, and to find the appropriate attribute label (i.e., attribute name) for each group. For example, in Figure 2.6, the label "Author," the textbox, the three radio buttons and their values below the textbox all belong to the same logic attribute. The label "Author" is the name of the attribute.

Logical attributes are determined as follows. For each element e in a row, WISE-*i* Extractor heuristically finds the text either in the same row or in the two rows above the current row that is most likely to be the label of the logic attribute for e based on an association weight of the text with e computed using five heuristic measures. It groups e with this text. In the end, all related elements that are grouped with the same text and the text itself are considered to belong to the same logic attribute. The five heuristic measures are:

1. *Ending colon.* Attribute labels often end with a colon, while other texts rarely do. For example, in Figure 2.6, "Author" is the attribute label with an ending colon, but "Exact name" is not.

2. *Textual similarity of the element name and the text.* It is the similarity between the internal name of the element and the text.

3. *Distance of the element and text.* An attribute label and its elements usually are close to each other in a query interface. These relationships are captured in the IEXP. The distance of a text and an element is given by $dict = \frac{1}{|I_e - I_t|}$, where I_e and I_t are the position indexes of the element and the text in the IEXP, respectively.

4. *Vertical alignment.* An element and its associated attribute label may be placed into different rows with one row having the label and the row below it having the element. In this case, they are aligned vertically, i.e., they have the same visual position in their respective rows. For example, in Figure 2.1, the attribute label "From" is vertically aligned with its element.

5. *Priority of the current row.* The text in the same row of an element is given higher priority.

After logical attributes are identified, the *attribute analysis component* of WISE-*i* Extractor performs a series of analyses to extract more useful information about the attributes. These analyses are briefly reviewed below.

1. *Differentiate different types of fields.* WISE-*i* Extractor classifies the fields of a logical attribute into two classes: *domain fields* and *constraint fields*. For example, in Figure 2.6, the attribute

"Author" has a domain field (the textbox) and three constraint fields (the three radio buttons). Domain fields are used to specify domain values for the attribute while constraint fields enforce some constraints to domain fields. The following heuristic observations are used to build a classifier for classifying the fields of a logical attribute:

(a) Textboxes cannot be used for constraint fields.

(b) Radio buttons, checkboxes, or selection lists may appear as constraint fields.

(c) An attribute consisting of a single field cannot have constraint fields.

(d) An attribute consisting of only radio buttons or checkboxes does not have constraint fields.

WISE-*i* Extractor uses a Naive Bayesian classifier to classify the fields of a logical attribute. Each field is represented as a feature vector of four features: field name, field format type, field relative position in the field list, and field values.

2. *Identify the relationships and semantics of domain fields.* For an attribute with multiple *domain fields*, there is a need to identify how these fields are related and the semantic meaning of each field. For example, in Figure 2.2, the two domain fields of "Price range" represent a range with the first field for specifying the *lower bound* of the range and the second for the *upper bound*. Three types of relationships for multiple domain fields are considered by WISE-*i* Extractor and they are *group*, *range*, and *part*. Intuitively, the *group* type is easy to identify because the elements in *group* relationship are all checkboxes or radio buttons. Range type relationships can be identified by some widely used *range keywords and patterns* in internal names and values such as "between-and" and "from-to." The remaining relationships (i.e., non-group and non-range) are recognized to have *part* relationships. WISE-*i* Extractor employs two naïve Bayesian classifiers to identify the relationships and semantics of domain fields: one is for the relationships and the other for field semantics. For the relationship classifier, the domain fields of each attribute are represented as a vector of four features including attribute name, element internal names, field labels, and field values. *Group* and *part* are the two class labels of the classifier. For the field semantics classifier, each field is represented as a vector of five features including its attribute name, relationship with other domain fields, field label, field internal name, and field values.

3. *Derive meta-information of attributes.* WISE-*i* Extractor derives additional meta-information for each attribute, including *domain type, value type, default value*, and *unit* [He et al., 2007]. Four domain types are defined in the interface model of WISE-*i* Extractor: *range, finite* (with a finite number of possible values but no range semantics), *infinite* (textbox, but no range semantics), and *Boolean*. WISE-*i* Extractor uses a trained domain type classifier based on several features (attribute labels, element labels and internal names, attribute values and element format types) to classify the domain type of each attribute. Seven value types are recognized by WISE-*i* Extractor and they are *date, time, datetime, currency, id, number*, and *char*. Useful

information for identifying value type of attributes includes their labels, element internal names and values. Another piece of important information is the observation that the identical or similar attributes from different query interfaces in the same domain usually have the same value type. Using these features, WISE-*i* Extractor trains a value type classifier to determine the value type for each attribute. *Default values* may occur in a selection list, a group of radio buttons, and a group of checkboxes. They are easy to extract because they are always marked as "checked" or "selected" in the HTML source of search forms. A *unit* defines the meaning of an attribute value (e.g., *kilogram* is a unit for *weight*). Not all attributes have meaningful units (e.g., attributes author and title). WISE-*i* Extractor uses the feature vector (*URLsuffix*, *attLabel*, *elemLabels*, *elemNames*, *elemValues*) for each attribute to train a unit classifier for unit identification.

4. *Identify logic relationships.* A query submitted through a query interface can be formed in four possible ways: *conjunctive*, *disjunctive*, *exclusive*, and *hybrid*. WISE-*i* Extractor is the only extractor that considers disjunctive, exclusive, and hybrid attributes. It uses heuristic observations to build Naïve Bayesian classifiers to identify these types of attributes. For example, it uses keywords such as "and," "or" to identify conjunctive/disjunctive attributes. As discussed earlier, it also employs a domain label vocabulary to identify *exclusive attributes*.

2.3.2 RULE-BASED EXTRACTION

HSP, VisQIExt, and OPAL (ontology-based web pattern analysis with logic) [Furche et al., 2011] are three of the most representative rule-based extraction tools. They use the visual rendering of query interfaces to derive extraction rules. They develop rules that attempt to capture common Web design practices. For example, the label of a field is positioned above, left, or right of the field. VisQIExt and OPAL in addition use rules based on the styling information: e.g., the labels of the members of a group of fields have the same text-style.

Hidden Syntax Parser (HSP)

HSP is part of the MetaQuerier project [Chang et al., 2005], which aims to help users in finding and querying Web databases effectively and uniformly. Recall that HSP adopts *query condition patterns* as the query representation model. HSP assumes that a *hidden syntax* guides the presentation of interface components on a query interface. This *hidden syntax* is formalized into a *visual language*, which is described in a *2P grammar*. The grammar rules are based on common layout patterns and relative preferences between these patterns. The patterns are derived from pre-studied examples of query interfaces in different application domains. The 2P grammar (without considering the preferences) is a special instance of *attributed multiset grammar* [Golin, 1991], where a set of spatial relations capturing topological information (e.g., left, right) is used in productions. For example, the query pattern "Author" in Figure 2.6 is captured with the following productions:

1.   TextOp ←Left(Attr, Val) ∧ Below(Op, Val)
2.   Op ←RBList
3.   RBList ← RBU | Left(RBList, RBU)
4.   RBU← Left(radiobutton, text)
5.   Attr ←text
6.   Val ←textbox

The 2P grammar provides a general and extensible mechanism for describing query condition patterns. For instance, it allows expressing complex patterns upon simpler patterns. For example, pattern TextOp is constructed from simpler patterns Attr, Op and Val. In addition, it is easy to incorporate new patterns and new constraints, while leaving the parsing algorithm untouched. The grammar, however, is ambiguous; that is, a "string" (an interface) can be generated by the grammar in more than one way (i.e., the string admits more than one *parse tree*). This is not difficult to note. For example, the text "Number of passengers" in Figure 2.1, can be either the label of the field below it, which corresponds to the production TextVal ← Below(Attr, Val), or above it, i.e., TextVal ← Above(Attr, Val). Thus, the query interface in Figure 2.1 has more than one parse tree. There is no general procedure for converting an ambiguous grammar into an unambiguous grammar. Some ambiguities can be resolved by introducing preferences among the productions of the grammar. HSP uses precedence at a higher level: among condition patterns. For instance, we would prefer the former interpretation of "Number of passengers" (TextVal ← Below(Attr, Val)) over the latter (TextVal ← Above(Attr, Val)), although, in this case none of them is correct, because "Number of passengers" is the label of the group of fields below it.

In general, the parsers for visual languages follow a bottom-up exhaustive approach which explores *all* possible interpretations. Some interpretations are discarded early in the parsing process since they cannot lead to a complete parse tree. They are called *local ambiguities*. To avoid ambiguities and to achieve maximum interpretations for a query interface, HSP employs a *best-effort parsing* algorithm that on one hand uses the preferences among patterns to prune the wrong interpretations, and on the other hand discards the parse trees with local ambiguities.

The next extraction technique addresses many of the ambiguities in HSP by introducing additional abstractions (e.g., *semantic group of fields*) and a set of "commonsense design rules" about Web design practices. For instance, it hypothesizes that because the fields *Adult*, *Senior*, and *Child* belong to the same semantic group, their labels should have the same style and the same spatial orientation with respect with their fields. That is, there cannot be two fields in the group such that one has its label to its right and the other to its left. This homogeneity property about the labels of the fields in a semantic group can resolve the ambiguity of the text "Number of passengers" mentioned above. This label cannot be the label of the field *Adult* because it is placed above the field *Adult*, whereas the label of the field *Senior* is positioned to the right of the field, and this violates the homogeneity property of the labels of the fields in the group. This is also referred to as a "design contradiction."

VisQIExt – a Visual-based Query Interface Extractor

VisQIExt is a component of VisQI (VISual Query Interface Integration) system [Kabisch et al., 2010], a Web database integration system. The underlying representation of a query interface in VisQIExt is a schema tree with an arbitrary number of levels. The extraction of a query interface into a schema tree is guided by two main insights. First, it hypothesizes that certain geometrical patterns between the fields (horizontal/vertical lines) reveal the presence of semantically related fields in a query interface. Second, it draws a parallel between the layout of an ordinary document and the appearance of a Web query interface: the fields along with their labels are the content and the labels of the groups are the headings. A label of a group of fields, similar to a heading, should succinctly summarize the upcoming set of fields. For example, the label in Figure 2.1, "Where Do You Want to Go?" describes the purpose of the fields in the section it introduces. A user, thus, learns that the fields "From" and "To" represent the departure and arrival information, respectively. VisQIExt is based on nine general rules on query interfaces, which attempt to capture common Web design practices. These rules were drawn by empirical observations and are listed below:

Rule 0: Query interfaces are organized top-down and left-to-right.

Rule 1: Fields within an interface are organized in semantic units of information, i.e., groups.

Rule 2: A label is used to denote either the semantics of a field or of a group of fields, but not both.

Rule 3: If a field f with a label l_f belongs to a group g with label l_g, then the *text-style* of label l_f is different from the text-style of label l_g.

Rule 4: If a group g with a label l_g is a subgroup of a group G with label l_G, then the text-style of label l_g is different from the text-style of label l_G.

Rule 5: The labels of all the members of a group have the same text-style.

Rule 6: The orientation of a label of a field is either to the left, above, right, or below of the field. The label of a group is either above or to the left of the group.

Rule 7: The labels of all the members of a group have the same orientation.

Rule 8: Let G be a group and g be one of its subgroups. Suppose a label with text-style FS_1 is assigned to G and a label with a different text-style FS_2 is assigned to g, then for any group H and its subgroup h, the label assigned to H cannot have the text-style FS_2 when the label assigned to h has the text-style FS_1.

We provide a high-level description of the steps of the extraction algorithm employed by VisQIExt for a given query interface.

Tree of Fields:

An initial tree of fields, called *FT*, is generated based on the *order* and *alignment* of the fields in the rendered version of the interface. VisQIExt employs the following geometric patterns. If straight line segments are drawn between any two consecutive fields on the interface, then all these line segments form one connected curve. The curve consists of horizontal, vertical, and diagonal line segments. A horizontal (vertical) line segment corresponds to a set of fields laid out row-wise (column-wise) on the visual rendering of the query interface. Figure 2.7 shows the curve for the interface in Figure 2.1. The curve may also have a number of *inflection points*. An inflection point is a point on the curve where the curve changes direction. An inflection point marks either the end or the beginning of a semantic group of fields in the interface. For instance, in Figure 2.7, inflection point B marks the end of the group of fields "From" and "To" and point C marks the beginning of the semantic group "Departure Date." An inflection point is the geometric "evidence" that the designer finishes/begins the organization of a subset of fields into a group of semantically related fields. Hence, a horizontal/vertical line segment emphasizes the presence of a group of fields. For example, the line segment [C; D] denotes the group "Where Do You Want to Go?," while the vertical line segment [E; F] represents the group "Number of Passengers." An inflection point that joins a horizontal line with a vertical line segment is assigned to the group corresponding to the horizontal line segment since the fields on query interfaces are mostly row-wise organized. Thus, the field *Economy* is grouped together with the field *Business Class & Higher* and not with the fields *Adult*, *Senior*, and *Child*. Figure 2.8 shows the derived tree of fields for the running example. For example, an internal node was added for the groups of fields *From* and *To*.

Tree of Texts:

VisQIExt hypothesizes that a text token in a query interface has a *semantic scope*. Intuitively, this is the area of the interface which is characterized by the semantic meaning of the text. As an example, in Figure 2.9, the semantic scope of "When Do You Want to Go?" is the rectangular area that includes every text token and fields that are between the text itself and the text "Number of Passengers." The semantic scope of "Departure Date" includes the text and the three fields denoting month, day, and time of departure. The tree of texts, called *TT*, is inferred from the inclusion relationship between the rectangular areas defining the semantic scopes of texts on an interface: e.g., in Figure 2.9, the semantic scope of "When Do You Want to Go?" includes that of "Departure Date," thus the latter text is a child of the former text. The tree in Figure 2.10 represents the tree of texts derived from the query interface in Figure 2.1.

The texts with the same values for their style properties (e.g., font-color, background-color, font-size) are clustered together. The semantic scope of a text t is the maximal rectangle with the following properties: (1) its left-upper corner coordinates are the coordinates of the left-upper corner of the bounding box of text t; (2) it extends downward and to the right until the semantic scope of another text p in the same style cluster or the boundary of the interface is met. Let q be a text from a different style cluster than that of t. If the bounding box of t is included in the semantic scope of q then the semantic scope of t is included in the semantic scope of q. Note that the notion of semantic

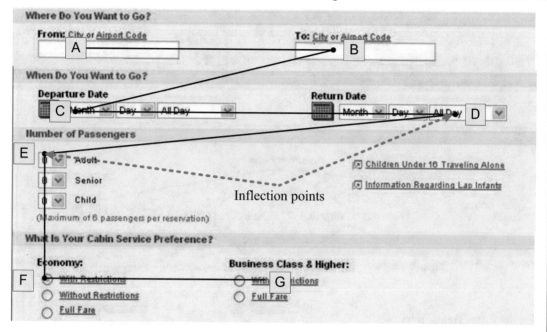

Figure 2.7: An example of horizontal/vertical lines and their inflection points.

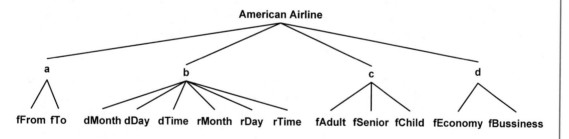

Figure 2.8: Tree of fields.

scope naturally follow from Rules 3, 4, and 5. Ideally, the tree of texts must reflect the property in Rule 8.

Candidate Labels for Fields:
Another important problem in the construction of the schema tree is the semantic tagging of its leaves (fields). There is no consistent pattern across query interfaces as to where a label is positioned with respect to the field. A label may be to the left, to the right, above, or below of the field. VisQIExt collects all possible candidate labels for each field and then, in the *integration* step (to be described

Figure 2.9: Label scope.

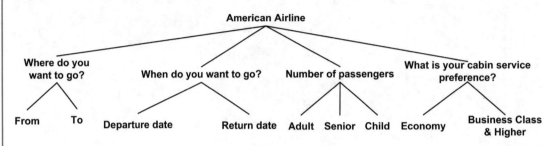

Figure 2.10: Tree of texts.

shortly), decides which are the appropriate ones. The candidate labels are collected according to Rule 6. A text token is chosen from the set of candidate labels as the final label, if it satisfies Rules 5 and 7. This process is applied iteratively, as whenever a final label is determined for a field, the set of candidate labels for every other field or group of fields is updated (Rule 2).

Integration:
The final hierarchical representation ST (schema tree) of the query interface is obtained by merging the two trees FT and TT. FT is the target tree and TT is the source tree. A directional "mapping" from TT to TF is defined. A label is mapped into a leaf (field) if it was determined to be a candidate label. The semantic scope of a label l contains a set of fields (leaf nodes). A label is mapped into an internal node if its semantic scope contains all the fields of the internal node. Multiple labels may be mapped into each node of the tree. New internal nodes may be added to the tree of fields FT. The goal of this step is to find the final schema tree and the assignment of labels to its nodes. For our running example, the final schema tree ST is depicted in Figure 2.4.

2.3.3   STATISTICAL LEARNING BASED EXTRACTION

LabelEx, HMME, and ExQ are the only statistical learning-based tools in the realm of Web query interface extraction. LabelEx employs supervised learning to assign labels to form elements. It designs a "Classifier Ensemble" using Naïve Bayes and Decision Tree classifiers. LabelEx uses textual and layout evidences to perform the text-label assignment task. HMME explores Hidden Markov Models for the task of query interface extraction. ExQ creates the interface structure tree using hierarchical agglomerative spatial clustering. Each form element is considered to be a visual attribute block. To generate the tree, spatially close and similarly styled blocks are clustered under the same internal node. ExQ performs node label assignment using annotation rules. Hence, ExQ is a hybrid query interface extractor. We describe HMME next.

HMME—A Hidden Markov Model Interface Extractor

The representation model in HMME is a two-level hierarchy model of the form [*attribute-name*, *operator*, *operand*]. HMME uses the layout and textual properties of elements. It accomplishes three tasks: text-label assignment, grouping, and semantic labeling. Semantic labeling corresponds to tagging the elements of an interface as one of *attribute-name*, *operator*, or *operand* categories. HMME views the interface design process as a stochastic process for laying out a *stream* of interface elements with different semantic roles. That is, it hypothesizes that there is a *hidden* process generating a stream of *observable* tokens (interface elements) with *unobserved* semantic roles. The goal thus is that of discovering their semantic roles and grouping them accordingly. The Hidden Markov Model (HMM) is a statistical tool for modeling generative sequences that can be characterized by an underlying process generating an observable sequence. An HHM is given by $\lambda = (A, B, \pi)$, where A is the transition matrix storing the probability of state j following state i; B is the observation array storing the probability of observation k being produced from state j; and π is the initial probability array. HMME adopts an HMM of first order, i.e., the current state depends only on the preceding state and the observable output depends only on the current state. Figure 2.11 gives the transitions of decoding the semantic roles of the elements in the query interface in Figure 2.6. In the figure, an oval represents a state and a rectangle represents an observable token. The dotted line signifies that the previous pattern of states is repeated two more times, to capture the logic attributes Title and Subject. In the figure, attribute-name "emits" text, operator "emits" a radio button group, and operand "emits" a textbox. After an HMM is learned to simulate the process, it is then used to automatically tag the elements of new interfaces.

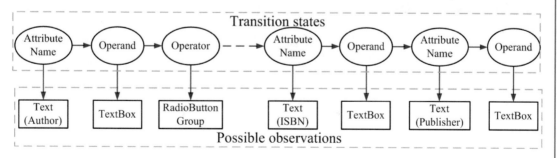

Figure 2.11: Decoding of interface in Figure 2.6.

HMME uses a two-layered HMM. The first layer, called T-HMM, tags the elements of a query interface with their corresponding semantic roles, and the second layer, called S-HMM, creates groups of related elements. Their topologies are depicted in Figure 2.12. Their numbers of states are empirically determined. Besides the "Misc. text" state, the semantic roles of the states of T-HMM are self-explanatory. This state is to recognize pieces of texts such as "(Maximum 6 passengers per reservation)" in Figure 2.1, which are not the labels of any of the elements of a query interface. The state transition probabilities are learned from a training set of 50 query interfaces using the Maximum Likelihood algorithm. T-HMM and S-HMM share the same observation token space.

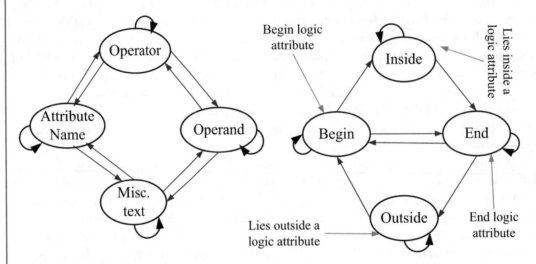

Figure 2.12: The topologies of T-HMM (left) and of S-HMM (right).

The input of S-HMM is the output of T-HMM. S-HMM completes the extraction task by determining the boundaries of logical attributes and tagging the elements with respect to their sequential position in a logical attribute.

C H A P T E R   3

Query Interface Clustering and Categorization

In order to provide a unified access to multiple structured deep Web databases, the first two tasks are: (1) to discover the relevant Web databases, and (2) to cluster them into different groups such that those in the same group cover data in the same domain (e.g., provide the same type of products/services) and those in different groups are for data in different domains. Finding the right Web databases is a very challenging problem. For example, a scientist needing to locate Web databases with climate data may try to post a query, such as "climate databases," to a major search engine (e.g., Google, Bing). Google, for instance, returns over 60 million results for this query. Among them, some Web pages refer to climate databases, while the overwhelming majority of them refer to pages from journals, scientific articles, etc. The need to effectively guide users to the appropriate Web databases has motivated some Web sites to undertake the arduous task of manually compiling online directories, which list and categorize Web databases. For example, the Molecular Biology Database Collection [Galperin, 2005] is an academic effort to list databases of value to biologists, while `www.completeplanet.com` and `www.invisibleweb.com` are commercial deep Web directories. The advantage of manual classification is the development of high quality directories. Nonetheless, because the Web is so vast and dynamic (new sources are constantly added, while existing sources are modified or even removed from time to time), a manual endeavor in organizing the Web databases is not feasible.

Organization of Web databases by their domain is also an important preliminary step toward supporting *Web database selection* (by finding Web databases of the same domains) and *query mediation* (by finding Web databases with similar query attributes).

The problem of deep Web source discovery is also an important part of the general deep Web content collection problem, which consists of three subtasks [Olston and Najork, 2010]:

1. *Locate deep Web sources.* A human or crawler must identify websites containing query interfaces that lead to Web databases.

2. *Select relevant sources.* For a certain domain (e.g., used car inventories), one must make a decision about which subset of the available Web databases to include in a Web database integration system. To enable this task, it is essential to construct a model of the contents available in a Web database.

3. *Extract underlying contents.* A crawler must extract the contents lying behind the query interfaces of the selected deep Web sources.

According to Olston and Najork [2010], locating deep Web sources is almost trivial for major search engines, since they possess a comprehensive crawl of the surface Web, which, in turn, is likely to include a large number of the query interface pages of Web databases. This may explain the limited work that has been done on this topic [Barbosa and Freire, 2007b; Bergholz and Chidlovskii, 2003; Liu et al., 2004]. Subtasks 2 and 3 pose significant challenges. There is also limited work on source profiling for Web databases [Dasgupta et al., 2010; Jin et al., 2011; Wang et al., 2004; Zhang et al., 2011], and little has been done that specifically pertains to crawling. Content extraction (Subtask 3) is the core problem in deep Web crawling [Fang et al., 2007; Liu et al., 2011; Madhavan et al., 2008; Raghavan and Garcia-Molina, 2001; Wang et al., 2008; Wu et al., 2006a; Zhang et al., 2011]. It consists of two main challenges: deciding which form inputs to fill when submitting queries via a query interface and finding appropriate values to fill in the inputs of a query interface. The latter is particularly difficult for textboxes (without features such as auto-completion) because, in general, no domain information is provided. This chapter does not cover the content extraction problem. It covers only issues pertaining to deep Web source discovery and textbox domain discovery. The former is an important preliminary step for clustering and categorization of deep Web sources, whereas the latter pertains to the query interface understanding problem.

In this chapter, we first discuss issues related to deep Web source discovery in Section 3.1. In Section 3.2, we cover different techniques for query interface clustering. In Section 3.3, we introduce methods for query interface categorization.

3.1 DEEP WEB SOURCES DISCOVERY

A key requirement for integration of deep Web sources is the ability to locate these sources on the Web. That is, to discover the *search forms* (i.e., query interfaces) that serve as entry points to their Web databases. The task is challenging because these forms are sparsely distributed over the Web. For example, a topic-focused crawler [Chakrabarti et al., 1999] retrieved only 94 Movie search forms after having crawled 100,000 pages related to movies. Consequently, a crawler, while it needs to search a broad area of the Web, still needs to avoid visiting large unproductive regions of the Web.

Inevitably, crawling the Web for deep Web data sources leads to a diverse set of HTML forms, many of which do not point to relevant deep Web sources. For example, it may lead to forms that require personal information (e.g., username, login information) or forms with textbox inputs. The latter are typically used with feedback inputs, e.g., comment submission forms on forums. As a result, an important task in deep Web source discovery is to separate the search forms from non-search forms. Another important problem is to locate deep Web sources in a given domain. Finally, once the sources of interest are discovered, we need to be able to interact with them (i.e., post meaningful queries). A key impediment in automatic interaction with these sources is the presence of textboxes on their query interfaces, which lack predefined set of values. Hence, domain discovery for textboxes becomes an important problem. The problem is critical for query interface understanding in general, because the knowledge of domains for textboxes enhances our ability to provide better solutions to a broad range of applications, such as identifying mapping between the attributes in different hidden databases and adding auto-completion feature to textboxes in integrated query interfaces, so as to improve their usability. This section presents solutions to these problems.

3.1.1   SEARCH FORMS VERSUS NON-SEARCH FORMS

Query interfaces have structural characteristics that are good indicators in determining whether or not an HTML form is a search form [Barbosa and Freire, 2007a]. It has been observed for example that search forms of deep Web sources have on average a larger number of selection lists and checkboxes than textboxes, whereas the reverse is true for non-search forms. Besides these features, a number of other structural features can be used to differentiate these two types of forms [Barbosa and Freire, 2007a], including the number of hidden tags, the number of radio tags, the number of file inputs, the number of submit tags, the number of image inputs, the number of buttons, the number of resets, the number of password tags, the number of textboxes, the number of items in selection lists, the sum of text sizes in textboxes, the submission method (*post* versus *get*), the presence of certain keywords, such as "search" and "find." HIFI [Barbosa and Freire, 2007a], a query interface classification tool, uses these features to build a number of classifiers, out of which, the decision tree (C4.5) classifier obtains the lowest error rate (9.5%) in separating search forms from non-search forms.

3.1.2   LOCATE DEEP WEB SOURCES

As mentioned above, little work has been conducted on this topic, particularly, for locating (structured) deep Web sources with complex query interfaces. In this section, we describe ACHE (Adaptive Crawler for Hidden-Web Entries) [Barbosa and Freire, 2007b]. Given a set of Web forms that are entry points to Web databases in a certain application domain (e.g., car rental), ACHE aims to efficiently and automatically locate other forms in the same domain. ACHE is a learning-agent-based approach and its architecture is shown in Figure 3.1.

The *page classifier component* is trained to classify Web pages as belonging to topics in a taxonomy (e.g., book, movies, and jobs). If ACHE retrieves a page that is classified as being on-topic, its query interfaces and links are extracted.

The *link classifier component* is trained to identify links that are likely to lead to Web pages that contain search forms. The classifier is trained off-line from a set of URLs of Web pages that contain query interfaces in the domain. It analyzes the *backlinks* from the training pages (e.g., this can be obtained using the Google API). The backward crawling is performed in a breadth-first manner. The documents at level $l + 1$ consist of all documents that point to documents at level l. The backward paths are manually inspected and a set of features is selected. The features are used to train classifiers that estimate the distance between a link and a page containing a search form. Intuitively, a link that matches the features of level l is likely l steps away from a page that contains

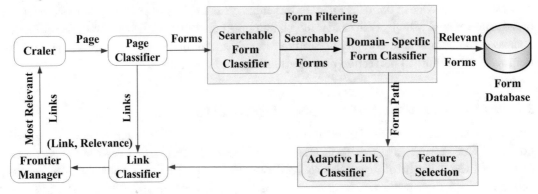

Figure 3.1: The architecture of ACHE.

a search form. This component adds the links to the *frontier manager component* in the order of their *predicted reward.*

The *frontier manager component* maintains a set of N priority queues with links that are yet to be visited. Each queue corresponds to a link classifier level. A link is placed in queue i if it is estimated that the link is i steps away from a target page. Links within a queue are ordered based on their likelihood of belonging to the level associated with the queue. At each crawling step, ACHE selects the link with the highest priority.

The *search form classifier component* filters out non-search forms. This classifier is domain-independent and was described in Section 3.1.1.

The *adaptive link learner component* uses features extracted from the successful paths gathered during the crawl to re-rank all links in the frontier manager component. To facilitate the learning, ACHE maintains a repository of successful paths. This component is invoked periodically, for example, after the crawler visits a pre-determined number of pages, or after it is able to retrieve a pre defined number of relevant forms. It is built using the Naive Bayes model.

The *feature selection component* extracts features (terms) present in the anchor, URL, and text around links that belong to paths which lead to relevant forms. The anchor feature set is constructed by first collecting all content words from the anchor itself, the n terms occurring before the anchor and the n terms occurring after it. The most frequent terms in this set constitute the feature set. The URL feature space is constructed by collecting the k most frequent terms appearing in the URLs of pages with relevant query interfaces.

The *form filtering component* is responsible for identifying, among the set of all forms retrieved by the crawler, the forms that belong to the target domain. ACHE uses HIFI [Barbosa and Freire, 2007a], a query interface categorization algorithm, to identify query interfaces that belong to a certain domain. Query interface categorization is discussed in Section 3.3.

3.1.3   GENERATING INPUT VALUES FOR TEXTBOXES

A large number of query interfaces have textboxes. A major challenge facing query interface matching and content extraction from deep Web repositories is the pervasive lack of data instances for textboxes. Several solutions have been proposed to discover values for textboxes [Jin et al., 2011; Madhavan et al., 2008; Raghavan and Garcia-Molina, 2001; Wu et al., 2006a]. In this section, we present the solutions proposed in the WebIQ [Wu et al., 2006a] and Google's Deep Web Crawl [Madhavan et al., 2008] systems, because they work in general settings and are motivated by different problems. The former is motivated by the query interface-matching problem, while the latter by the deep crawling problem. The solution analyzed by Jin et al. [2011], while relevant, works in a restricted setting, which we describe briefly now.

Let X be the set of input textboxes of a query interface and Y the rest of the input elements of the interface. Assume $X \neq \emptyset$. Suppose that there exists at least one valid query submission using only the input elements in Y, i.e., all the inputs in X are left empty (or with their default values). With this assumption, seed values for the attributes in X are obtained by analyzing the result pages returned in response to queries posted using only the input elements in Y. While many deep Web sites (e.g., `nsf.org`) return valid answers to such queries, many others sources do not. For example, many websites in the airfare domain use a textbox for the "Departure location" attribute. If a value is not provided for this attribute, the website returns an error page. This technique is not applicable to these kinds of deep Web sources. For Web sources that satisfy the above constraints, this work however provides a very comprehensive study of the problem of estimating the domain of a textbox input element by issuing the least amount of queries to the underlying website.

WebIQ Approach

Most solutions for matching attributes of query interfaces exploit the similarity between their names (i.e., labels of attributes) as well as that between data instances. Matching attributes with no instances is very challenging since we can only rely on their names, which are often generic or similar to many other names. For example, in Figure 3.2, the name of attribute B_1, "Departure city," is similar to that of both A_1 ("From city"), a matching attribute, and A_2 ("Departure date"), a non-matching attribute. Consequently, it is important to develop solutions that discover data instances for the attributes of query interfaces, as these solutions can significantly improve the interface matching accuracy. WebIQ [Wu et al., 2006a] proposes a solution that learns from both the surface Web and the deep Web to automatically discover instances of textboxes. WebIQ proposes two solutions for finding instances for a textbox: (1) discover instances from the surface Web, and (2) borrow instances from other attributes.

Discover Instances from the Surface Web

Given a textbox A, WebIQ first extracts the label L of A. If L is a noun or noun phrase then L is used to formulate an *extraction query* such as "*departure cities* such as." The extraction query is submitted to a search engine and the returned snippets are analyzed for candidate data instances for

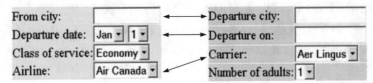

Figure 3.2: Two query interfaces in airfare domain.

A. The extraction queries can be regarded as incomplete sentences, and the "job" of the search engine is to complete the sentences with instances. The formulation of an extraction query is based on a set of generic extraction patterns. Figure 3.3 provides some examples of extraction patterns. Each extraction pattern consists of two parts: *cue phrase* (shown in italic) and *completion* (NP or NP_i's). For example, the cue phrase in s_1 is "Ls such as," where Ls is the plural form of the label L, and the completion is a list of noun phrases $NP_1,\ldots, NP_n$, each considered to be an instance candidate for the textbox. For example, one such query is Q = "*departure cities* such as." WebIQ examines the snippets in the result pages to extract candidate instances. Figure 3.4 shows a snippet for query Q. WebIQ extracts four instances from this snippet: New York, Chicago, Los Angeles, and Baltimore. WebIQ has an extraction rule for each extraction pattern.

s_1: *Ls such as* $NP_1, \ldots, NP_n$
s_2: *such Ls as* $NP_1, \ldots, NP_n$
s_3: *Ls includes* $NP_1, \ldots, NP_n$
s_4: $NP_1, \ldots, NP_n,$ *and other Ls*

Figure 3.3: Example extraction patterns (L: label, Ls: L's plural form, NP: noun phrase).

<u>Mucho Travel Deals to Sunny Mexico in Summer | Frommers.com</u>
www.frommers.com › Deals & News
May 12, 2005 – Additional **departure cities, such as** New York ($849), Chicago ($759),
Los Angeles ($655) and Baltimore ($1039) are available. The prices ...

Figure 3.4: A result snippet from Google.

Once a large enough set of instances is collected for a textbox *A*, WebIQ validates whether an instance x is a true instance of *A*. The validation attempts to assess the semantic connection between the candidates and the attribute, based on their co-occurrence statistics on the surface Web. If x is indeed an instance of attribute *A*, it expects the label of *A* to frequently co-occur with x. For each instance candidate x of textbox A, WebIQ forms several *validation queries* using some validation patterns as shown below:

1. *proximity-based*, e.g., "L x." For example, this pattern gives "departure city Chicago" as the validation query for L = "departure city" and x = "Chicago."

2. *cue phrase-based* such as the pattern "Ls such as x." For example, "departure city such as Chicago" is a validation query formed by this pattern.

Let V be a validation phrase and x an instance candidate. Let $V + x$ be the validation query. WebIQ computes the PMI (*pointwise mutual information*) [Salton and McGill, 1983] between V and x:

$$\frac{NumHits(V+x)}{NumHits(V) \times NumHits(x)} ,\qquad(3.1)$$

where $NumHits(V)$ and $NumHits(x)$ are, respectively, the numbers of hits obtained from a search engine on the validation phrase and the instance candidate, and $NumHits(V + x)$ is the number of hits on the validation query. If multiple validation queries are employed, then the confidence score of x being an instance of A is taken to be the average of PMI scores for x. The top-k candidate instances are retained.

Borrow Instances from Other Attributes

Suppose that b is an instance of attribute B. WebIQ tries to verify if b can also be an instance of the attribute A. The verification can be done via the surface Web or the deep Web. The verification via the deep Web is relatively straightforward: a probing query is formulated by setting the value of A to x and the values of other attributes to their default values. Then it analyzes the response page from the source and determines if the submission was successful.

To verify if instances of B can be instances of A via the surface Web, WebIQ first learns an instance classifier for A from a training set, then employs the learned classifier to classify the instances of B. The training of the classifier is fully automatic, with no need for manually prepared training examples. Additional details can be found from the work by Wu et al. [2006a].

Google's Deep Web Crawl Approach

While the previous technique was motivated by the query interface-matching problem, this method is motivated by the content-extraction problem. The Google's deep Web crawl (GoogleDeep-Crawl) [Madhavan et al., 2008] classifies textboxes into two classes: *generic* and *typed*. Examples of typed textboxes are *date*, *price*, and *zip code*. The motivation for distinguishing between these two types of textboxes arises from a pragmatic observation: It is observed that there are relatively few types that appear in many search forms and, thus, can be used to index many domains. The two types are handled differently by GoogleDeepCrawl. For a typed textbox, the problem is to determine its type from a predefined set of types, which includes both discrete (e.g., U.S. states) and continuous (e.g., price) data types. GoogleDeepCrawl uses the so-called *distinctness fraction* measure to determine the appropriate type of a textbox. That is, for each textbox, a number of predefined types are considered, say $T_1, T_2, \ldots, T_n$. T_i is one of the types such as price, U.S. states and zip code. For each type T_i, a sample set G_i of values is available. It inputs each value in G_i to the textbox and submits the query to the underlying deep Web site. Let $S_i = \{Sig(p) | p \in G_i\}$, where $Sig(p)$ is a function that computes signatures for HTML pages. (While $Sig(\bullet)$ is not explicitly defined by Madhavan et al. [2008], Google does hold a patent on a document duplicate detection method[7], which is likely to have been used in this work.) The distinctness fraction for T_i is $\frac{|S_i|}{|G_i|}$. The type recognized for a textbox is the one whose distinctness fraction is the highest and is at least 0.3. This threshold is experimentally determined. If the best distinctness fraction is less than 0.3, then the type of the textbox is deemed unrecognized and is treated as generic. Note that the lower bound for the distinctness fraction is $\frac{1}{|G_i|}$, because in the worst case each query submission returns the same result page (e.g., a page with the message "No result found for the query …"). The distinctness fraction is 1 if each query submission with a value from G_i returns a distinct result page.

For generic textboxes, GoogleDeepCrawl uses an iterative probing approach to identify the candidate values (keywords). It starts from an initial seed set of words as values for the textbox and constructs queries with the textbox while the rest of the input elements are set to their default values. It extracts additional candidate words from the resulting pages. The extracted words are used to update the candidate values for the textbox. The process is repeated until either it is unable to extract further words or has reached an alternate stopping condition. On termination, a subset of the candidate words is chosen as the set of values for the textbox. We now describe the details for the seed set of keywords and the selection of the candidate keywords.

GoogleDeepCrawl selects seed words from two sources: from the terms appearing on the search form page, and from the terms of the pages generated by the form submissions. It uses the TF-IDF [Salton and McGill, 1983] measure to identify the words in a page most relevant to its contents. The TF-IDF measure of a term t in a document d from a document collection D is the product of the *term frequency weight* (*tfw*) and the *inverse document frequency weight* (*idfw*) of t, where the former is a function of the term frequency (*tf*) of t in d (e.g., $tfw(t, d) = 1 + \log tf_{t,d}$, with $tf_{t,d} > 0$ being the number of times t appears in d; $tfw(t, d) = 0$ when $tf_{t,d} = 0$) and the latter is a function of the inverse of the document frequency (*df*) of t in D (e.g., $idfw(t) = \log(N/df)$, where N is the number of documents in D and *df* is the number of documents in D that contain t). For the seed words, it selects the top $N_{initial}$ words on the form page sorted by their TF-IDF scores.

For the candidate words at iteration $i + 1$, suppose that W_i is the set of all result pages generated and analyzed until iteration i. Let C_i be the set of words that occur in the top N_{probe} words on any page in W_i. GoogleDeepCrawl eliminates from C_i words that (1) appear in only one page in W_i or (2) have appeared in a large fraction of the pages in W_i (say 80%). The former set of words corresponds to words that are not representative of the content of the deep Web site, while the latter very likely corresponds to words that occur in advertisements, menus, etc. The remaining words in C_i are the candidate words for iteration $i + 1$. $N_{initial} = 50$ and $N_{probe} = 25$ are experimentally shown to be good values to extract sufficient candidate words for a generic textbox.

---

[7] www.google.com/patents/US7627613.

3.2   QUERY INTERFACE CLUSTERING

There are two general methods of query interface clustering: *Pre-query* and *Post-query* [Ru and Horowitz, 2005]. Post-query uses probe queries and the retrieved results to identify content belonging to a domain to accomplish clustering. Keyword-based query interfaces, which usually consist of a single textbox HTML element, are relatively easy to fill out automatically. It is however significantly more difficult to apply this technique to complex multi-attribute query interfaces, because it is more difficult to formulate queries on these interfaces [Madhavan et al., 2008; Wu et al., 2006b]. Pre-query relies solely on visible features in query interfaces and their hosting Web pages. In this subsection we discuss mostly the pre-query clustering techniques.

A number of query interface clustering algorithms have been developed [Noor et al., 2011]. They can be distinguished by the type of data they employ for clustering and by their underlying clustering approach. Most of them use feature vector spaces extracted from the query interfaces themselves [Barbosa et al., 2007; He et al., 2004b; Le and Conrad, 2010; Lin et al., 2008; Mahmoud and Aboulnaga, 2010; Nie et al., 2008; Zhao et al., 2008]. A few others explore richer feature spaces. For instance, some extract feature spaces from the Web pages hosting the interfaces [Barbosa and Freire, 2007a; Barbosa et al., 2007; Le and Conrad, 2010; Lu et al., 2006], while others employ pre defined topic hierarchies [Su et al., 2006b]. The clustering algorithms can also be broadly classified into supervised [Barbosa and Freire, 2007a; Nie et al., 2008; Su et al., 2006b; Xu et al., 2007b] and unsupervised [Barbosa et al., 2007; He et al., 2004b; Lu et al., 2006; Mahmoud and Aboulnaga, 2010; Xu et al., 2007a; Zhao et al., 2008] clustering algorithms.

Virtually all clustering methods for Web databases are based on features extracted from HTML pages hosting the query interfaces. Since these features are shared among the clustering algorithms, we start this section with their enumeration. When we describe the clustering algorithms, we will mention which set of features each algorithm uses. The clustering algorithms described in this section are characterized along the following three dimensions: (1) the input data, (2) the clustering objective function, and (3) the underlying clustering approach.

3.2.1   CLUSTERING FEATURES

The following are features that can be extracted from the Web pages containing query interfaces of Web databases [Lu et al., 2006].

1. *Page content feature space* (*PC*). This feature represents the query interface page (i.e., the Web page containing the search form) feature space and it consists of all distinct terms appearing in the interface page, other than those appearing in the query interface. For example, in the Web pages of digital camera stores, there usually are some terms specific to cameras, such as "Kodak," "Olympus," "Resolution pixel," or "LCD," while the Web pages selling cars may have terms like "Honda," "Ford," "Model," "Make," or "Engine." The *vector space model* [Salton and McGill, 1983] is the underlying model for this feature space. The TF-IDF measure is used to weight the importance of the terms. With this weighting model it is expected that terms unique to a

domain have higher weights (e.g., "flight," "departure," and "destination" have high frequencies within the Airfare domain but rarely appear in other domains), whereas generic terms have lower weights (e.g., "shop," "privacy").

2. *Form name feature space* (*FN*). *FN* consists of all distinct terms appearing in a query interface. For example, the query interfaces of book search engines usually have attribute names such as "title," "author," "ISBN," and "category," while those of automobile search engines usually have names such as "model" and "make." The name terms on a query interface are good indicators of the contents of the Web databases and are very useful for clustering Web databases. The terms on a query interface can also be represented as a vector of terms with weights. The weights can be computed using the TF-IDF formula. An interface may contain many textual pieces besides the names of its attributes, e.g., "Children Under 16 Travelling Alone" in Figure 2.1 (Chapter 2). A variation of this feature space is when only the terms in the names of the attributes are considered. We refer to this vector space as the *form name terms* (NT). Note that this feature space requires that the schemas of all query interfaces to be extracted (see Chapter 2).

3. *The number of images* (*NI*). This feature is useful for differentiating deep Web sources that sell tangible products from those selling intangible products. Tangible products are those that have a physical presence such as books and music CDs while intangible products such as insurance policy have no physical presence. The query interfaces of sources that sell tangible products usually have more images than those that sell intangible products. The reason is that Web sources selling tangible products tend to display their products to attract customers (as the saying goes: "A picture is worth a thousand words"), but Web sources selling intangible products have no physical product to display. Images that are decoration labels, buttons, or icons are ignored. These images can largely be detected by their sizes (can be obtained from the width and height attributes of images) and the ratio of width to height of the images.

4. *Form value terms* (*FV*). Many form elements have predefined values. For example, in the book search form of `amazon.com`, the name "Format" is implemented using a selection list which has values like "hardcover," "paperback," and so on. The purpose of these values is to allow users to specify more precise queries than using just keywords. In many cases, the form field labels alone cannot represent the real meanings of their associated fields. For example, both automobile and book search engines usually have an attribute labeled "category." However, in book search engines, "category" has such values as "art," "history," "novel," etc, while in automobile search engines, "compact car," "SUV," "truck" are some of its common values. Thus, the values of attributes are also important indicators of the contents of a search engine. The form value terms in a query interface can also be represented as a vector of weighted terms. Again, the weights can be computed using the TF-IDF.

5. *Price terms* (*PT*). For online shopping customers, price information is very important for their purchase decisions. To attract consumers, bargaining products or top-selling products

are frequently advertised with prices on the interface pages of Web databases that sell tangible products. Products of the same category usually have similar prices. As such, the range of price values can be useful to differentiate different types of products. For example, the typical price range of a book is between $5 and $25 and usually does not exceed the price of a digital camcorder, whose price typically ranges from $200 to $1700. It is easy to identify prices as they are usually associated with some currency symbols, such as Dollar "$," Yuan "¥," and Pound "£." Price values cannot be compared directly for matching purposes. For example, values 19.95 and 19.99 are very close even though they are different. To facilitate meaningful matching, each price can be converted to a *representative price* that is then used for comparison. Each representative price represents all prices within a certain price range. For larger prices, the range should also be larger. This is because a $10 difference is much more significant for low-price items than for high-price items. The following function can map an original price P to a representative price P' (it is a slightly revised version from the one used by WISE-Cluster [Lu et al., 2006]):

$$P' = \begin{cases} 5, & if \quad P < 10 \\ \lceil P/m - 0.5 \rceil * m, m = 10^{\lfloor \log P \rfloor} & if \quad P \geq 10 \end{cases}. \tag{3.2}$$

This function maps any price less than 10 to 5. For any price $P \geq 10$, let P be denoted by $c \times 10^k$, where $1 \leq c < 10$ is a real value and $k \geq 1$ is an integer. Then $m = 10^k$ and $P' = \lceil c - 0.5 \rceil \times 10^k$. The ceiling effectively helps the above function map prices in a certain range to the same price value. As an example, when $P = 16.99 = 1.699 \times 10$ (i.e., $c = 1.699$ and $k = 1$), $m = 10$ and $P' = \lceil 1.699 - 0.5 \rceil \times 10 = 20$ can be obtained from the above function. In fact, all prices in the range $(15, 25]$ will be mapped to the same representative price value 20. The range grows larger for higher prices, reflecting the fact that the prices of more expensive items fluctuate more in absolute values. For instance, all prices in $(1500, 2500]$ will be mapped to 2000 using Formula (3.2). Representative prices are referred to as *price terms* hereafter. The price information in an interface page is represented as a vector of price terms with weights. If the prices are in different currencies, then they need to be converted to prices in the same currency before their representative prices are generated.

3.2.2 SCHEMA (METADATA)-BASED CLUSTERING

In this section we describe two clustering algorithms, MD_{hac} [He et al., 2004b] and BinaryLT-HAC [Mahmoud and Aboulnaga, 2010], whose inputs consist only of information extracted from the query interfaces and nothing else.

MD_{hac} Algorithm
Query interfaces are represented as *query schemas*, i.e., attributes in their query interfaces. For example, $Q_1 = \{\text{"title,"} ..., \text{"price range"}\}$ is the query schema of the query interface in Figure 2.2 (Chapter 2) and $Q_2 = \{\text{"make,"} ..., \text{"price"}\}$ is the query schema of the query interface in Figure 2.5 (on the

right). Query schemas can be extracted with one of the algorithms described in Chapter 2. The input of MD_{hac} is provided by the HSP extraction algorithm [Zhang et al., 2004]. MD_{hac} views a schema as a *transaction* (e.g., with items {"make,",…, "price"}). Because a transaction is a special case of categorical data, MD_{hac} is an instance of the clustering algorithms for categorical data. MD_{hac} is a *model-based* clustering algorithm. That is, intuitively, it hypothesizes that similar schemas are generated by the same *hidden (generative) model* and thus they should be clustered together; whereas dissimilar schemas are generated by different hidden models, hence they must be placed in different clusters. The hidden generative model probabilistically generates schemas from a finite vocabulary of attributes (see the discussion in Section 2.1.2). MD_{hac} defines a *model-differentiation* objective function, which seeks to maximize the statistical heterogeneity among clusters. MD_{hac} uses the general hierarchical agglomerative approach (HAC) for clustering [Liu, 2007]. More details about the algorithm are described below.

Formally MD_{hac} views the problem of clustering of query interfaces as follows. The population of interest consists of G clusters with each cluster generated by a different model. Let $X = \{\mathbf{x}_1,…\mathbf{x}_n\}$ be a set of schemas, where each $\mathbf{x}_i$ is independently generated from one of the G models, $M_1, … , M_G$. The probability of generating $\mathbf{x}_i$ in the kth model is $\Pr(\mathbf{x}_i|M_k)$. A clustering of X is a partition of X into G groups: denoted by $(X; P) = (C_1,…, C_G)$, where P partitions X. The objective of model-based clustering is to identify the partition P such that all $\mathbf{x}_i$'s generated from the same model $\Pr(\bullet|M_k)$ are placed into a single group.

We now define the generative model for query interface schemas. Suppose that we have a universe of attributes. Then a (randomly picked) schema in a domain corresponds to a sampling *without replacement* [Casella and Berger, 2001] from the universe of attributes. For example, a schema with n attributes corresponds to an experiment with n trials, in which once an attribute is selected, it cannot be selected again. This model, while accurate, has difficult homogeneity testing for clusters. MD_{hac} approximates this generation model with a *sampling with replacement* model. In this strategy, to generate a schema from a cluster, the model of the cluster is a *multinomial probability model*. That is, a multinomial model for a cluster C consists of an exhaustive set of N mutually exclusive events (the events correspond to the attributes) $A_1, … , A_N$ (the set of all observed attributes in C) with associated probabilities $p_1, … , p_N, p_1 + … + p_N = 1$. Denote the model by $M = \{A_1 : p_1, … , A_N : p_N\}$. The probability of generating an attribute A from M is

$$\Pr(A|M) = \begin{cases} p_i, & \text{if } A = A_i \\ 0, & \text{otherwise} \end{cases}. \tag{3.3}$$

Note that this model may generate schemas with duplicate attributes, e.g., {"make," "make," "model," "price"} in the Auto domain. However, according to He et al. [2004b], this does not create problems in practice. Under this model, a schema Q with n attributes is viewed as $Q = \{A_1 : y_1, … , A_n : y_n \}, y_1 + … + y_n = n$, where y_i represents the frequency of attribute A_i in Q. For a query interface, y_i is either 0 or 1, i.e., there are no duplicate attributes in an interface. The probability of generating schema Q from model M is

$$\Pr(Q|M, n) = n! \prod_{i=1}^{N} \frac{\Pr(A_i|M)^{y_i}}{y_i!} . \tag{3.4}$$

A cluster of schemas $C = \{Q_1, \ldots, Q_m\}$, where schema Q_i has n_i attributes, is seen as an experiment with $n_1 + \ldots + n_m$ trials. In other words, C is seen as a series of samplings from the same multinomial distribution M. Therefore, C is viewed as $C = \{A_1 : z_1, \ldots, A_N : z_N\}$, where z_i is the sum of all the frequencies of the attribute A_i among the schemas in the cluster C.

Example 3.1 Let C be a cluster with four schemas: $Q_1 = \{A, B, E\}$, $Q_2 = \{A, B\}$, $Q_3 = \{A, D, E\}$ and $Q_4 = \{A, E\}$. The universe of attributes has 4 attributes: A, B, D, and E. Under the multinomial model, a schema is a set of attribute frequencies, e.g., $Q_3 = \{A:1, B:0, D:1, E:1\}$ and $C = \{A:4, B:2, D:1, E:3\}$. The probability of generating Q_3 is

$$\begin{aligned} \Pr(Q_3|M, 3) \quad &= 3! \frac{\Pr(A|M)^1}{1!} \times \frac{\Pr(B|M)^0}{0!} \times \frac{\Pr(D|M)^1}{1!} \times \frac{\Pr(E|M)^1}{1!} \\ &= 6 \Pr(A|M) \Pr(D|M) \Pr(E|M). \end{aligned}$$

The objective function of clustering is some function H that characterizes the heterogeneity of models under a partition P, denoted by $H(X; P)$. The goal of clustering is to find the partition P that maximizes function H, where H is constructed as follows. Suppose that there are m clusters $C_1, \ldots, C_m$, each generated from its own multinomial distribution. Suppose that there are n attributes $A_1, \ldots, A_n$. Construct a contingency table O such that O_{ij} represents the frequency of attribute A_j in cluster C_i. Let $X_i = \sum_{j=1}^{n} O_{ij}$, $Y_i = \sum_{i=1}^{m} O_{ij}$ and $S = \sum_{i=1}^{m} X_i = \sum_{j=1}^{n} Y_j$. Define the random variable

$$D^2(C_1, \ldots, C_m) = \sum_{i=1}^{m} \sum_{j=1}^{n} \frac{(O_{ij} - X_i \times \frac{Y_j}{S})^2}{X_i \times \frac{Y_j}{S}} . \tag{3.5}$$

It can be shown that D^2 has an asymptotic χ^2 distribution with $(n-1)(m-1)$ degree of freedom (df). The objective function used in MD_{hac} is

$$H(C_1, \ldots, C_m) = \frac{D^2(C_1, \ldots, C_m)}{D_s^2(df)} , \tag{3.6}$$

where $D_s^2(df)$ is the normalization factor and it is the value of D^2 at significance level 0.5%.

A few observations are in order regarding the derivation of the above objective function. First, from statistics, we know that χ^2 testing can be used to test the homogeneity among multiple clusters by constructing a contingency table when the clusters follow multinomial distributions. Thus, the random variable $D^2(C_1, \ldots, C_m)$, which is asymptotically χ^2 distributed, can be used to test the homogeneity among the clusters. $D^2(C_1, \ldots, C_m)$ was obtained by constructing a contingency table. This works because the clusters are generated from multinomial distributions. Second, $D^2(C_1, \ldots, C_m)$ cannot be used alone because its values for different degrees of freedom need to be comparable. Hence, we normalize $D^2(C_1, \ldots, C_m)$ by $D_s^2(df)$.

Recall that MD_{hac} adopts the general HAC clustering approach. That is, in each iteration, the pair of most similar clusters is merged, and the process is repeated until only G clusters remain. The similarity measure between two clusters C and C' in MD_{hac} is $H(C, C')$ (Formula 3.6). In general, HAC starts by placing each data point (schema) in a singleton cluster. However, MD_{hac} cannot start by placing each schema in a singleton cluster because of the way the objective function is defined. The value of H is affected if D^2 does not closely converge to χ^2 distribution. It is known that the χ^2 test requires that each event (attribute in our setting) to have at least five observations to ensure a good approximation of χ^2 distribution [Casella and Berger, 2001]. Therefore, MD_{hac} has a pre-clustering phase in which schemas are deterministically grouped. The grouping is performed using the *anchor attributes*, which are those attributes that are only observed in one domain. For example, "make" and "model" are anchor attributes for the Auto domain, whereas ISBN and "author" are anchor attributes for the Books domain. The grouping may still produce some groups with insufficient observations and, thus, these groups cannot be considered in the iterative clustering process. These are called *loner groups*. A loner group has the property that the sum of the frequencies of all the attributes occurring in the group is lower than a threshold (it is conventionally set to 5). MD_{hac} also has a post-clustering step, in which each schema Q in a loner group is added to the cluster C with the highest $\Pr(Q|M, n)$ (Formula 3.4), where n is the number of attributes in Q.

BinaryLT-HAC

The premise of this algorithm is that in general we have no way of automatically determining with absolute certainty if two given Web databases belong to the same domain. Consequently, this algorithm takes a probabilistic approach for handling uncertainty in clustering. That is, a Web database is placed into multiple clusters (domains) with different probabilities. The probability that two Web databases belong to the same domain is determined based on the textual similarity between the attribute names of their query interfaces. Therefore, this algorithm uses the NT (*form name terms*) vector space. However, instead of the TF-IDF weighting model, it uses a binary vector of features to represent a query interface: one feature for each distinct term to indicate whether a term exists among the names of the elements of the interface. The feature vectors are created as follows. Let $S = \{S_1, \ldots, S_m\}$ be the schemas of a set of query interfaces for which a clustering is sought. We first collect all distinct content terms (i.e., stop words are ignored) appearing in the attributes of all query interfaces. Then we sort them into a vector of terms N. For each $S_i \in S$ we create a feature vector F^i whose dimension equals to that of N. The jth feature of F^i is 1 if $\max_{t \in T_i} tsim(t_j, t) \geq \tau$; otherwise is 0. In $\max_{t \in T_i} tsim(t_j, t) \geq \tau$, T_i is the set of terms occurring in the attributes of S_i, t_j is the term in the jth entry of N, *tsim* is a function that takes two terms as input and returns a real value in the range $[0, 1]$ that indicates how similar the two terms are and τ is an empirically set threshold. Given two terms t and t', the function that computes their similarity is given by:

$$tsim(t, t') = \frac{2len(LCS(t, t'))}{len(t) + len(t')} , \tag{3.7}$$

where $len(t)$ is the number of characters in t and $LCS(t,t')$ denotes the longest common substring between t and t'.

BinaryLT-HAC also is a hierarchical agglomerative clustering and it needs two similarity measures: one between two schemas and the other between two clusters. The similarity between two query interfaces $S_i, S_j \in S$ is computed using the Jaccard coefficient:

$$ssim(S_i, S_j) = Jaccard(F^i, F^j) = \frac{|\{r : F_r^i = r \wedge F_r^j = r\}|}{|\{r : F_r^i = r \vee F_r^j = r\}|} , \tag{3.8}$$

where F_r^i is the rth component of the vector F^i. All pair-wise query interface similarities are computed and stored before commencing clustering to avoid recomputing them multiple times during clustering.

If we denote by $U^{(k)}$ the set of clusters at the beginning of the kth iteration of the algorithm, the similarity between two clusters $U_i^{(k)}, U_j^{(k)} \in U^{(k)}$ is defined as the average of the similarities between every schema in $U_i^{(k)}$ and every schema in $U_j^{(k)}$:

$$csim(U_i^{(k)}, U_j^{(k)}) = \frac{1}{|U_i^{(k)}||U_j^{(k)}|} \sum_{S_a \in U_i^{(k)}} \sum_{S_b \in U_j^{(k)}} ssim(S_a, S_b) . \tag{3.9}$$

Initially, every schema is considered a singleton cluster. Then the HAC algorithm proceeds iteratively by merging the most similar pair of clusters (according to Formula 3.9) among the set of clusters into one new cluster. The algorithm stops when the similarity of any pair of clusters is no larger than a threshold δ, which is empirically set. Let the last set of clusters produced when the algorithm stops be $C = \{C_1, \ldots, C_n\}$.

At this point each Web database belongs to one and only one cluster in C. In the next step, the algorithm attempts to assign a Web database to multiple clusters (domains) with different probabilities if it has sufficient similarity to each of them. Let the set $D = C$ be an exact copy of the set of clusters obtained in the previous step. We need D because all the computations in this phase of the algorithm are performed with respect to the set of clusters produced by the previous step, i.e., C, whereas the assignment is performed with respect to D. The elements of D are called *domains* to distinguish them from those in C. In order to accomplish this task, BinaryLT-HAC requires a measure of similarity between a query interface and a cluster. Given a cluster $C_r \in C$ and a query interface $S_i \in S$, their similarity is defined as:

$$scsim(S_i, C_r) = \frac{1}{|C_r|} \sum_{S_j \in C_r} ssim(S_i, S_j) . \tag{3.10}$$

For a schema S_i to be assigned to a domain D_r, two conditions must be satisfied: (1) $scsim(S_i, C_r) \geq \delta$ and (2) $\frac{scsim(S_i, C_r)}{\max\limits_{C_j \in C} scsim(S_i, C_j)} \geq 1 - \theta$, $\theta \in [0, 1]$ (θ is set experimentally to

0.02 [Mahmoud and Aboulnaga, 2010]). This parameter quantifies the degree of uncertainty of assigning a Web database to multiple domains. The lower the θ is the more confident we are about assigning S_i to D_r. The probability that S_i belongs to D_r is $scsim(S_i, C_r)$ normalized so that all the probabilities assigned to S_i sum up to 1. For this purpose, we need to define two sets. The first is $D(S_i)$, which is the set of domains in D such that S_i satisfies (1) and (2). The second set is $S(D_r) = \{S_j | D_r \in D(S_j)\}$. Then the probability that S_i belongs to D_r is:

$$\pi_{ir} = P(S_i \in D_r) = \begin{cases} \dfrac{scsim(S_i, C_r)}{\sum\limits_{D_j \in D(S_i)} scsim(S_i, C_j)}, & \text{if } S_i \in S(D_r) \\ 0, & \text{otherwise} \end{cases} . \qquad (3.11)$$

This phase of BinaryLT-HAC outputs triplets of the form $\langle S_i, D_r, \pi_{ir} \rangle$, $D_r \in D$ and $S_i \in S$. This is the final output of the algorithm BinaryLT-HAC.

3.2.3   VOCABULARY-BASED CLUSTERING

The effectiveness of the previous clustering techniques highly depends on the accurate extraction of query interfaces (e.g., field labels), which, as discussed in Chapter 2, is a task that is hard to automate. We describe here two methods for clustering Web databases: CAFC-CH [Barbosa et al., 2007] and WISE-Cluster [Lu et al., 2006]. CAFC-CH does not require query interfaces to be extracted, whereas WISE-Cluster still needs to extract query interfaces. Nevertheless, WISE-Cluster utilizes many other features besides those derived from the schemas of query interfaces (e.g., *PT* and *NI*). In that regard, WISE-Cluster is a hybrid clustering approach, because it utilizes both schema-based and vocabulary-based features. Both techniques utilize the features available on the interface page, such as the text terms appearing in the interface page, or the number of images shown in the interface page [Lu et al., 2006]. These approaches essentially cast the problem of Web database categorization into a document clustering problem. This approach seems to be more robust and general because it is able to handle a wide range of query interfaces, including single-field query interfaces and interfaces with little or no descriptive textual elements.

CAFC-CH Clustering Algorithm

This algorithm uses only the *FN* and *PC* feature spaces. Both *PC* and *FN* are texts. Each of them has an associated vector $\overrightarrow{PC}$ and $\overrightarrow{FN}$, respectively. A Web database is associated with a form page *FP*. An *FP* is a triplet (*Backlink*, $\overrightarrow{PC}$, $\overrightarrow{FN}$), where Backlink consists of a list of URLs that point to *FP*, $\overrightarrow{PC}$ is the page content feature vector and $\overrightarrow{FN}$ is the form name term feature vector. $\overrightarrow{FN}$ consists of the weights of all the distinct terms appearing in the query interface in *FP*, while $\overrightarrow{PC}$ consists of the weights of all the distinct terms appearing in the interface page. An expanded TF-IDF weighting scheme is used to compute the importance of each term. This scheme takes into consideration the location of a term in a query interface page. The weights of term i in a query interface page P for both the *FN* and *PC* feature spaces are computed as follows:

$$w_i = LOC_i \times TF_i \times \log\left(\frac{N}{n_i}\right),$$ (3.12)

where LOC_i is a small integer whose value depends on the location of term i in P, N is the total number of interface pages under consideration and n_i is the number of interface pages that contain term i. TF_i is the frequency of term i in P.

The *Cosine* similarity measure [Salton and McGill, 1983] is employed to compute the similarity between the vectors of two different interface pages. The similarity of two interface pages P_1 and P_2 are combined by taking the weighted average of their $\overrightarrow{PC}$'s and $\overrightarrow{FN}$'s:

$$sim(P_1, P_2) = \frac{w_1 \cos(\overrightarrow{PC_1}, \overrightarrow{PC_2}) + w_2 \cos(\overrightarrow{FN_1}, \overrightarrow{FN_2})}{w_1 + w_2}.$$ (3.13)

In CAFC-CH, w_1 and w_2 are set to 1.

Backlink explores the similarity based on the existence of common ancestors for interface pages. The backlinks can be obtained from the hyperlink structure of interface pages. Clustering of interface pages by backlinks follow the intuition that the existence of an ancestor pointing to a set of pages $P_1, P_2, \ldots, P_n$ is an indication that these pages may be related (similar).

The clustering algorithm CAFC-CH is a two-step algorithm. In the first step, clusters are derived based on the backlinks structure of interface pages. This step deterministically clusters the interface pages. That is, interface pages with the same ancestor are considered similar and placed in the same cluster. These clusters become the seed clusters for the second step. The second step is a K-means clustering algorithm that uses Formula (3.13) to cluster similar pages. Specifically, each cluster has two associated (centroid) vectors: one for $\overrightarrow{PC}$ and the other for $\overrightarrow{FN}$. The centroid vector of a cluster C is computed by taking the average of the weights of the terms in different interface pages in C:

$$\vec{c} = \left(\frac{\sum\limits_{\overrightarrow{PC} \in C} \overrightarrow{PC}}{|C|}, \frac{\sum\limits_{\overrightarrow{FN} \in C} \overrightarrow{FN}}{|C|}\right).$$ (3.14)

The algorithm iterates over the interface pages, assigning each interface page to the cluster whose centroid is most similar to it. The process is repeated until the clusters become stable. CAFC-CH iterates until fewer than 10% of the interface pages move across clusters.

One problem of the backlink-based clustering is that it produces too many clusters. For the second step to be effective, we need to identify the K most representative clusters. From the set of all clusters produced in the first step, the clusters that contain only intra-site information are discarded. These clusters have the property that all the backlinks belong to the same site as the interface page that is being clustered. These clusters do not add much information about the topic of the interface page. From the remaining set of clusters, K clusters are selected such that they are the K most distant clusters. A greedy strategy is utilized to select them. Let S be the set of seed clusters. Initially, $S = \emptyset$. We first add to S the two most distant clusters. The distance between two clusters is computed with Formula (3.13). A new cluster C is appended to S if the sum of the distances between C and the clusters in S is maximal.

WISE-Cluster Algorithm

WISE-Cluster uses all the features described in Section 3.2.1 to cluster query interfaces. The similarity between two query interfaces is the weighted sum of the similarities between the PC vectors, the FN vectors, the FV vectors, the PT vectors, and the number of images (NI) of the two query interfaces, respectively. More specifically, for two Web pages containing two query interfaces S_1 and S_2, let $simNI(S_1, S_2)$, $simFN(S_1, S_2)$, $simFV(S_1, S_2)$, $simPT(S_1, S_2)$, and $simPC(S_1, S_2)$ be the similarities between S_1 and S_2 based on their numbers of images, form term vectors, form value term vectors, price term vectors, and interface page term vectors, respectively, and let $sim(S_1, S_2)$ be the overall similarity between S_1 and S_2. The following formula is used to compute $sim(S_1, S_2)$:

$$
\begin{aligned}
sim(S_1, S_2) = {}& w_1 \times simNI(S_i, S_2) + w_2 \times simFN(S_1, S_2) \\
& + w_3 \times simFV(S_1, S_2) + w_4 \times simPT(S_1, S_2) \\
& + w_5 \times simPC(S_1, S_2) ,
\end{aligned}
\tag{3.15}
$$

where weight coefficients w_1, w_2, w_3, w_4, and w_5 are determined by a genetic algorithm based method [Lu et al., 2006]. The similarity between two feature vectors is computed using the *Cosine* similarity function.

Let N_1 and N_2 be the numbers of images in the query interfaces of S_1 and S_2, respectively. Then $simNI(S_1, S_2)$ is defined as:

$$
simNI(S_1, S_2) = 1 - \frac{|N_1 - N_2|}{\max\{N_1, N_2\}} .
\tag{3.16}
$$

WISE-Cluster also is a two-step clustering algorithm. In the first step, it uses a supervised K-means clustering algorithm. K is the number of clusters. It assumes that K is known beforehand. For example, it suggests that a list of domains can be compiled in advance (e.g., for products, the domains can be obtained from the Yahoo category "Business and Economy $\rightarrow$ Shopping and services") and K can be assigned the number of domains in the list. This step consists of two phases. In the first phase, it manually selects one query interface for each domain and assigns it to the corresponding cluster. Even though manual effort is needed in this phase, it is a one-time effort (unless new product domains appear). In the second phase, for each of the remaining query interfaces, the K-means algorithm is applied, i.e., we compute its similarity with every cluster and assign it to the most similar cluster. The similarity between a query interface S and a cluster C is defined as the average of the similarities between S and every query interface in C. After the preliminary clustering step, those clusters that still contain only the manually assigned query interfaces are discarded. In other words, the initial K used is allowed to be larger than the actual number of domains among the input query interfaces.

In the second step, WISE-Cluster moves potentially unfitting query interfaces from their current clusters to more suitable ones. This is carried out as follows. (1) It computes the average similarity (AS) of each cluster C, which is the average of the similarities between all interface pairs in cluster C. (2) It identifies every interface S in C whose $sim(S, C)$ is less than AS. These query interfaces are considered to be potentially unfitting as their similarities with the cluster are below the average similarity of the cluster. (3) For each S obtained in Step (2), the algorithm computes its similarities with all current clusters (including the cluster that contains S) and then moves it to the cluster with the highest similarity. Note that if S has the highest similarity with the cluster that contains S in the first place, then S will not be moved. The average similarity of cluster C is updated incrementally, i.e., immediately when a query interface is removed from or added into it, rather than at the end of processing all unfitting query interfaces of C. The above refining process is repeated until there is no improvement (increase) on the sum of the similarities of all clusters.

3.3 QUERY INTERFACE CATEGORIZATION

In this section we discuss the task of assigning each query interface to an appropriate concept (i.e., domain name), possibly in a concept hierarchy. In general, the classification task can be accomplished in two ways. In the first method, we first cluster the interfaces (e.g., using one of the algorithms described in Section 3.2) and then assign each cluster to a concept. In the second approach, the task of clustering and that of classification are conducted at the same time by first choosing a pre defined set of concepts from a concept hierarchy, train a classifier for each concept in the hierarchy, and then classify new query interfaces into the concept hierarchy using the learned classifier(s). With the exception of the work by Lu et al. [2006], all existing classification methods fall into the second approach. We will refer to them as *supervised domain-assisted classification methods*.

The domain concepts can be generic with a limited number of general domain concepts, such as movie, book, or music. But they can also be more detailed, including more specific categories. For example, a book category can be divided into subcategories such as cooking books, art books, science books, etc. The benefit of the latter is that specialized deep Web sources (e.g., `allrecipes.com`, `www.artbook.com`) can be more appropriately classified than with using generic concepts. With the exception of the method by Nie et al. [2008], all the other classification techniques consider general domain concepts.

3.3.1 CLUSTER ASSIGNMENT

In this subsection we discuss the task of assigning each cluster (domain) to an appropriate concept. The discussion is based on the methodology used in WISE-Cluster [Lu et al., 2006]. There are two motivations for performing this step. First, by assigning a cluster to an appropriate concept, we can use the concept to name the cluster. This can be useful for summarizing the result of the clustering. Second, cluster assignment can serve as a mechanism to adjust the initial clusters based on the concepts preferred by an application. Clusters formed using the algorithms described in Section 3.2 are independent of any specific applications. A particular application may sometimes require the merge of some basic clusters into a single cluster. For example, suppose that by using one of the aforementioned clustering algorithms, a cluster for "insurance" and a cluster for "investment" were generated. But a particular application is interested in clusters corresponding to higher-level concepts such as "financial service" (e.g., the concept hierarchy for the application does not have concepts "insurance" and "investment" but only "financial service" and other high-level concepts). Through the process of assigning basic clusters to appropriate concepts in a given concept hierarchy and merging the clusters assigned to the same concept, application dependent clusters may be generated from application independent clusters.

To assign clusters to concepts, we first generate a representative for each cluster and a representative for each concept in the hierarchy, and then match the representatives. The following explains how the representatives are generated.

The representative of a cluster is its centroid. Specifically, the representative of a cluster is a vector of features represented as (NI, NT, FV, PT, PC), where each feature is the average of the corresponding features of all the query interfaces in this cluster. For example, each component in the form name term vector (NT) of the centroid is the average of the corresponding components in the form name term vectors of all query interfaces in the cluster. The weight of a term t in any term vector is computed based on the following TF-ICF formula:

$$\left(0.5 + 0.5 \times \frac{tf}{\max\_tf}\right) \times \log \frac{N}{cf} \, , \tag{3.17}$$

where cf is the cluster frequency of t (i.e., the number of clusters that contain t) and N is the number of clusters. The reason that icf is used is because the more clusters a term appears in, the less useful the term is in differentiating different clusters.

The representative of each concept is obtained as follows. For each concept c, k interfaces that belong to this concept are selected and assigned to c for some small integer k (WISE-Cluster uses $k = 3$). In other words, each concept is represented by a small cluster of k interfaces. Then the centroid of each such cluster is computed and is used as the representative of the concept.

When assigning a query interface cluster to the concepts, the algorithm first computes the similarity between the representative of this cluster and the representative of every concept using Formula (3.15), and then assigns the cluster to the concept with the highest similarity value.

3.3.2   SUPERVISED DOMAIN-ASSISTED CLASSIFICATION METHODS

In this subsection, we introduce a supervised pre-query [Le and Conrad, 2010] and a supervised post-query [Su et al., 2006b] classification techniques. Most of the classification techniques (e.g., Barbosa and Freire, 2007b; Le and Conrad, 2010; Xu et al., 2007b) use a mere enlisting of Web database domains, e.g., {auto, book, hotel, music, job, airfare, movie, car rental}; others (e.g., Su et al., 2006b) use a manually predefined concept hierarchy for Web databases. The HIFI method [Barbosa and Freire, 2007a] is a supervised domain-assisted method. Its underlying technique is CAFC-CH, which was described earlier in Section 3.2.3. Several other methods pertain to this category [Nie et al., 2008; Su et al., 2006b], and they employ query probing for classification. Among them, we briefly cover the solution proposed by Su et al. [2006b].

SVM with Feature Selection Classification Algorithm
In this algorithm [Le and Conrad, 2010] each query interface is treated as a bag-of-words. This technique uses the feature spaces *PC* and *FN*, plus the words extracted from the titles (i.e., the words appearing between the <title> tags) of query interface pages. Words are not stemmed because of the observation that words such as "book" in Airfare domain and "books" in the Book domain must be seen as two different discriminative features and not merged by stemming them. The algorithm regards the problem of query interface classification as a document categorization problem. The algorithm is as follows. Let $C = \{c_1, \ldots, c_n\}$ be the set of categories and $D = \{d_1, \ldots, d_m\}$ be the training set of query interfaces. Each interface $d \in D$ is labeled with a predetermined category $c \in C$. Let V be the set of all features (i.e., content words) appearing in D. Let d^* be a new query interface not in D that is to be classified into some category in C. The algorithm has the following steps:

1. Use a feature selection method to select from V a subset V_{FS} of features. V_{FS} will be used by the algorithm. Let $|V_{FS}| = N$.

2. Represent each interface $d \in D$ according to the feature vector V_{FS}. Let $v = (w_0, \ldots, w_{N-1})$ be the vector representation of d. v is a binary vector of features. That is, $w_j = 1$ if the term t_j is in d; $w_j = 0$ otherwise.

3. Use an SVM with a linear kernel classifier. The classifier is trained from the m vectors associated with the query interfaces in D. The output is the pre defined domain categories.

4. After the learning process is completed, the SVM classifier can be used to classify the new query interface d^*.

The feature selection procedure has the following steps. First, it computes a score for each term $t \in V$, according to a scoring function to be defined shortly. Second, it assigns to each term (feature) t the category c with the maximum $P(c|t)$, where $P(c|t)$ is the conditional probability that a random query interface containing the feature t belongs to the category c. Third, it sorts the terms in each category by their scores in descending order; then it re-ranks all terms together first by the relative ranks in their categories in ascending order and second by their scores in descending order. Finally, it selects the top-N ranked terms from the set of all terms, where N is a parameter determined through a cross-validation procedure. The scoring function, called *top-to-category separation* (T2CS), is defined as follows:

$$T2CS(t) = [P(t|c_1) - P(t|c_2)] \times [P(c_1, t) - P(c_2, t)], \qquad (3.18)$$

where c_1 and c_2 denote the two categories that have the first and the second highest values of all probabilities $P(c_i, t)$ for $i = 1, \ldots, n$; $P(t|c_1)$ is the conditional probability that a random interface in category c_1 contains feature t.

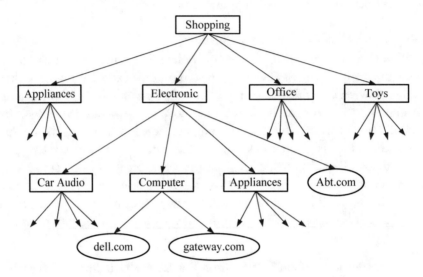

Figure 3.5: Example of a concept hierarchy.

Hierarchical Classification of Deep Web Databases

An alternative way to tackle the problem of classifying query interfaces is to assume the existence of a predefined concept hierarchy for Web databases. For training purposes, we also need a number of human-classified Web databases at each node of the concept hierarchy. This assumption is reasonable considering that there are some commercial directories, such as CompletePlanet (www.completeplanet.com), already available. Figure 3.5 illustrates such a hierarchy. In the concept hierarchy in Figure 3.5, categories have rectangular shapes, whereas Web databases are represented using oval shapes. Some machine learning algorithms can be used to learn classifiers that given a new Web database find the appropriate concept (node) in the hierarchy that represents the Web database. An example of this technique is the method described by Su et al. [2006b]. Since this method works only with simple query interfaces (i.e., with just a simple keyword textbox), we only give a brief overview of this method.

For each training database, a set of probing queries is constructed from the associated titles (names) of hierarchy nodes. For example, if the title is "Art," then the query "Art" is submitted to each Web database under the node "Art" in the hierarchy. The query result counts returned by the training databases are used to train and construct an SVM classifier for each internal node of the concept hierarchy. For example, if a database reports "Your search for Art matches 159 records," then the record count is 159. The counts may need to be normalized because different Web databases have different numbers of records. For example, `amazon.com` has millions of books, while `artbook.com` has only several tens of thousands of books. When a new database needs to be classified, the same set of probing queries is submitted to the database and the SVM classifiers are utilized to classify the new database into the hierarchy. The classification method traverses the hierarchy top-down starting from the root and pushes the new Web database as low as possible in the hierarchy.

CHAPTER 4

Query Interface Matching

Schema matching is defined as the task of discovering semantic correspondences between attributes across Web query interfaces. It is a necessary step for query interface integration. Consider the two query interfaces in the airfare domain in Figure 4.1. We can see that attribute *Depart City* in the interface on the left corresponds to attribute *Leaving from* in the interface on the right. While the correspondences of fields between the two query interfaces in Figure 4.1 are obvious for a human being, it is not so for an automated matching system. For instance, the system must understand that *Depart City* is semantically equivalent to *Leaving from* and that *Adult* and *Child* together correspond to *Passengers*. The former correspondence is an example of a 1:1 (one-to-one) matching, i.e., one attribute in an interface is equivalent to one attribute in another interface, whereas the latter is an example of a 1:m (one-to-many) matching, i.e., one attribute in an interface is equivalent to multiple attributes in another interface. Schema matching is responsible for determining these semantic correspondences.

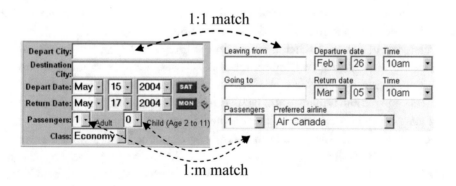

Figure 4.1: Illustrating 1:1 and 1:m semantic matches.

A distinctive feature of the query interface matching techniques over the traditional ones (e.g., schema matching between pairs of relational schemas) is that they consider schema matching "holistically" by matching many schemas at the same time and finding all matchings at once. The holistic approach relies on large data volumes to discover semantic correspondences of attributes. Therefore, these techniques employ data mining methods. From this angle, they can be classified into *statistical model discovery* [He and Chang, 2003], *clustering* [He et al., 2003; Wu et al., 2004], and *correlation mining* [He et al., 2004a; Nguyen et al., 2010; Su et al., 2006a; Wang et al., 2004] approaches.

This chapter is organized as follows. In Section 4.1, a brief overview of the traditional schema matching is provided. In Section 4.2, the unique challenges of query interface matching are reviewed. In Section 4.3, clustering-based matching approaches are presented. In Section 4.4, the statistical model discovery and the correlation mining approaches are described. In Section 4.5, techniques that mainly employ data instances to perform the matching task are covered.

4.1   TRADITIONAL ATTRIBUTE MATCHING

Query interface integration has its root in *database schema integration*. As a result, some techniques developed for database schema integration can be applied to or adopted for certain aspects of query interface integration. Database schema integration aims to construct an *integrated schema (global schema)* from a set of existing or local schemas [Batini et al., 1984; Parent and Spaccapietra, 1998; Ram and Ramesh, 1999]. Such an integrated schema is useful for supporting unified access to multiple databases from a single database schema. For example, in heterogeneous or multidatabase systems, an integrated schema can be constructed to support unified access to multiple autonomous database systems possibly in different data models (e.g., relational, object-oriented, etc.) [Sheth and Larson, 1990]. In this book, we assume that all local input schemas are in the same data model—the relational data model. Otherwise, schema transformation is performed to transform input schemas not in the same data model to schemas of the desired data model.

The first step of database schema integration is *schema matching*, which is to identify corresponding *schema elements* (e.g., attributes, relations, classes, etc.) across multiple local database schemas. In this section, we provide a brief review of schema matching techniques in traditional database schema integration. Other steps of database schema integration such as attribute integration and schema merging will be reviewed in later chapters (Sections 5.1 and 6.1).

Database schema matching has been extensively researched and several surveys and summaries of the main techniques can be found in the literature (e.g., Bellahsene et al., 2011; Rahm and Bernstein, 2001; Shvaiko and Euzenat, 2005). Database schema matching is usually carried out between two schemas. There are two levels of matching granularity—*element-level* and *structure-level* [Rahm and Bernstein, 2001]. *Attribute matching* is an example of matching at the element-level granularity and *relation matching* is an example of a structure-level matching as each relation has a structure, i.e., a set of attributes. An example of a more complex structure-level matching is a matching of one relation in one schema with two relations in another schema (e.g., *Students* in one schema matches *Graduate_Students* and *Undergraduate_Students* in another schema) .

Element-level matching can be of 1:1 and 1:m mappings. Usually most matchings are of type 1:1, e.g., *Title of Book* in one schema matches *Title of Books* in another schema. An example of type 1:m matching is *Name of Employee* in one schema matches *First_Name* and *Last_Name* of *Staff* in another schema. When a 1:m mapping is identified, a *mapping expression* can be used to relate the involved elements. For example, *Name* can be expressed as a concatenation of *First_Name*, a space and *Last_Name*.

Attribute matching can be performed using different types of information which can be classified as *name-based*, *schema-based*, and *instance-based*. Two attributes may be matched by their names through exact match, synonym match (e.g., *Subject* and *Category* for books), hypernym/hyponym match (e.g., *Address* and *Home_Address* for employees), and approximate string matching (e.g., *Phone#* and *PhoneNo* for persons). One problem with name matching is the *homonyms*, which are names with the same or similar spellings but different meanings. For example, *Type* for employees in one schema may be used to indicate whether an employee is a salaried employee or hourly employee while in another schema it is used to denote whether an employee a full-time or a part-time employee. The existence of homonyms is one of the reasons that name-based techniques may fail sometimes. Note that name-based techniques can also be used to match relations for relational schema matching.

Schema-based techniques explore schema metadata created when an attribute is defined in a relation schema. Such metadata include the data type of an attribute, whether an attribute is a key (both primary key or unique key), whether it is a foreign key referencing the same or similar attributes, what check constraint is specified on an attribute, and whether null value is allowed for an attribute. Schema metadata are usually not strong enough by themselves for determining attribute matching, but when combined with other techniques such as name-based matching, they can provide additional evidence to improve attribute matching accuracy.

The values under attributes in populated relations can be utilized to help attribute matching. This is known as the instance-based method. When two attributes have common values (including synonyms) or their values have common patterns (e.g., their averages and ranges are similar for numerical values, whether their values can be characterized using the same or similar regular expressions such as those for phone numbers and email addresses, and whether their values are of the same type such as person names), then the two attributes are likely to match. The instance-based method can be very effective for identifying homonyms because homonyms usually do not have similar values.

In a general schema matching framework [Rahm and Bernstein, 2001], a number of matchers can be created with each performing match based on one type of information and then these matchers are combined to help draw an overall decision on whether two elements are matched. For attribute matching, individual matchers can be developed using name-based, schema-based, and instance-based techniques as described above. There are two general ways to combine individual matchers: *hybrid combination* and *composite combination* [Rahm and Bernstein, 2001]. The former directly combines multiple matchers into a single tightly coupled process (e.g., data type and value pattern are used at the same time when name-based matchers fail to reach a conclusion for a match) while the latter lets each matcher output its own decision (could be in the form of a matching score) and then combines the results (e.g., use weighted sum of individual matching scores or other aggregation techniques) to determine a final outcome of a match. Hybrid combination is usually more efficient as often not all matchers need to be executed for each pair of candidate elements (i.e., some matchers can be used as filters to determine whether additional matchers should be executed). But this method requires human experts to design and modify (e.g., to incorporate a new or improved matcher) the combination process. In contrast, composite combination is very flexible in terms of adding new or improved matchers or changing the result aggregation method.

In relational schema integration, the result of attribute matching can be used to facilitate relation matching. If two relations share some significant attributes (such as primary key, unique key, name, etc.), then they are more likely to be matched.

Query interface schema matching and traditional database schema matching share some common issues but also differ in many aspects. A relational database schema may have multiple inter-related relation schemas. Thus, there is a need for relation matching. In contrast, a query interface schema is like a single relation schema, and therefore, relation matching is not needed for query interfaces of Web databases in the same domain. Many similar features can be used for attribute matching for both database schema matching and query interface schema matching. These features include attribute name (label), data type, value type, etc. But they also have some unique features not available for the other. For example, whether an attribute is a key of a relation is available for a relation schema but not available for an interface schema. As another example, *domain type* information (e.g., whether an attribute has a finite number of values such as a selection list or an infinite number of values such as the case of textbox) is available for an interface schema but not for a relation schema. While most features for relation schemas are readily available, features for interface schemas need to be extracted from the interface pages. As pointed out earlier, another significant difference between traditional database schema matching and query interface matching is that the former usually considers two schemas at a time while the latter often considers many interfaces at the same time in a holistic manner. When query interfaces are represented as hierarchies of fields, interface schema matching also involves matching nodes or subtrees in multiple schema hierarchies. Query interface schema matching will be discussed in the remaining sections of this chapter.

4.2   QUERY INTERFACE ATTRIBUTE MATCHING CHALLENGES

We present, in this section, a number of challenges that make the query interface-matching problem a difficult endeavor. The key challenges include schema heterogeneity of query interfaces, attributes lacking data instances, and the presence of stop words in the attribute labels.

Schema Heterogeneity
The input of traditional schema matching consists of either relational or structured (e.g., XML) schemas. Names of attributes in those schemas correspond to internal names of attributes in query interfaces. The attributes of those schemas may be named in a highly inconsistent manner (e.g., using acronyms), imposing many difficulties in their correct matching. Query interfaces, on the other hand, are designed for user consumption and attribute labels are more meaningful and consistent. For example, the vocabularies of query interfaces in a domain tend to converge (Section 2.1.2).

Nevertheless, schema heterogeneity still persists. We provide here a number of examples along with the difficulties they pose to interface schema matching.

First, some labels are uninformative from a matching algorithm's perspective, such as *From* and *To* in Figure 4.2. The words of these labels are not present in electronic dictionaries (e.g., WordNet [Fellbaum, 1998]), and unless we have additional knowledge (e.g., data instances), it is very difficult to find their correct matches. For example, *From* is usually semantically equivalent to *Departure City* in the airfare domain, but this relationship is difficult to discover based on their terms alone. Second, some terms are ambiguous. For example, the term "departure" may appear in both *Departure Date* and *Departure City*. These terms may lead to false matches. Third, some fields do not have a label. They are either part of a larger concept (e.g., the field "month" in Figure 4.1 is part of the concept *Departure Date* together with the fields "day" and "year") or they are standalone concepts, in which case they almost always have data instances. These fields are also difficult to match. In the former case, unless we use a hierarchical representation of query interfaces (Section 2.2.2) and, thus, recognize that such a field belongs to a larger semantic group, we may not be able to find their proper matching. For instance, a field "month" appears in both the *Return Date* and *Departure Date* in Figure 4.1. If we use a flat representation for query interfaces, we may not be able to distinguish between the field "month" in *Return Date* and that in *Departure Date* and may derive incorrect matches by matching the field "month" in *Departure Date* to the field "month" in *Return Date* in Figure 4.1. These issues can be alleviated if query interfaces are represented hierarchically as to be shown later in this chapter (Section 4.3.1).

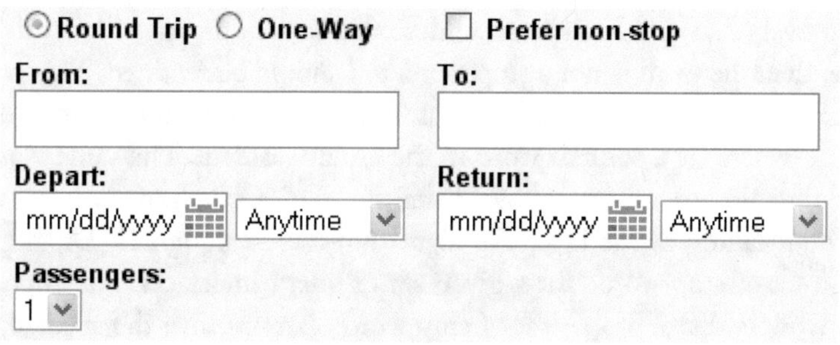

Figure 4.2: An example of a query interface with uninformative labels.

Finally, the same concept may be represented differently across query interfaces. For example, the concept of *Passengers* in the airfare domain is modeled as two fields *Adult* and *Child* in the interface on the left in Figure 4.1, whereas it is represented as a single field in the interface on the right in Figure 4.1. This is an example of a *complex match*. Complex matches are difficult to discover using only the metadata (e.g., labels, internal names, data instances) associated with the fields in query interfaces. We present in this chapter two techniques for discovering complex matches:

one uses correlation mining (Section 4.4.1) and the other uses clustering along with a number of heuristics (Section 4.3.1).

Lack of Instances

Another major challenge facing query interface matching is the pervasive lack of data instances (i.e., values). Query interfaces often contain many attributes with no instance at all, such as the attributes *Depart City* and *Leaving from* in Figure 4.1. In one study [Wu et al., 2006a] it was found that the percentage of attributes with no instance ranges from 28.1% to as high as 74.6% on the deep Web. In addition, in many cases, for attributes that have data instances the number of their instances is often small and even when the attributes match, their instances are often dissimilar. For example, the attributes *Preferred Airline* and *Carrier* match, but the former may list instances that are mostly North American airliners (e.g., Air Canada) and the latter may list mostly European airliners (e.g., Aer Lingus).

Stop Words

In information retrieval, the set of stop words is generic with possibly some adjustments. The identification of stop words in query interfaces can be tricky. For example, the words "from" and "to" in a query interface can denote an origin city and a destination city (see Figure 4.2), respectively, and their deletion would cause two attributes to have null labels, which is clearly unacceptable. Similarly, if in another query interface these two words are removed from the labels of the attributes "from city" and "to city," then the two attributes cannot be distinguished (i.e., the *homonym problem*). In general, if the removal of a word leads to an undesirable situation such as two attributes becoming indistinguishable, then the word is not a stop word and should be retained. This problem is further complicated because a stop word in one domain may not be a stop word in another domain. As an example, the word "where" is a content word in the airfare domain. The same word is a stop word in the credit card domain because its removal from the label "Cell phone [where] we may call you" does not affect the meaning of the label. An algorithm can be designed [Dragut et al., 2009b] to identify a suitable set of stop words for a given set of query interfaces. An important conclusion drawn from this work is that a proper set of stop words can improve the accuracy of determining semantic relationships among labels by as much as 33% than when a domain independent set of stop words is used and by as much as 43% than when no set of stop words is used.

4.3   CLUSTERING BASED ATTRIBUTE MATCHING

In this section we present two algorithms, one by Wu et al. [2004] and the other by He et al. [2003], which use clustering techniques to discover matching attributes across query interfaces. The former matching algorithm uses a hierarchical agglomerative clustering (HAC) algorithm to identify both 1:1 and 1:m matches. The latter algorithm is a two-step clustering algorithm and identifies only 1:1 matches. This algorithm is part of the WISE-Integrator [He et al., 2005], a system for extracting and integrating complex web search interfaces of the deep Web. We first present the algorithm by Wu et al. [2004] and then the one by He et al. [2003].

4.3.1 A HAC-BASED QUERY INTERFACE MATCHING

Given a set of user interfaces, each with a set of attributes that are hierarchical arranged (Section 2.2.2), the problem is to identify the attributes in one user interface that are equivalent to the attributes in other interfaces.

Recall from Section 2.1 that each attribute in a query interface is characterized among others by a label, an internal name, a set of instances, and the value type such as time, date, currency, area, and integer. In the HAC approach, each attribute A is represented by a vector $AV = (L, N, V, VT)$, where L, N, V, and VT stand for the label, the internal name, the set of instances and the value type of the attribute, respectively. In Figure 4.1, the attribute *Adult* has $L = $ "Adult," $N = $ "numAdult," $I = \{1, 2, ..., 9\}$, and $VT = $ the set of positive integers.

For two attributes A_i and A_j from different user interfaces, we compute their similarity by comparing their corresponding vectors:

$$sim(A_i, A_j) = sim\left((L_i, N_i, I_i, VT_i), (L_j, N_j, I_j, VT_j)\right) . \tag{4.1}$$

The similarity between two vectors can be obtained by computing the similarities of the four components and then take a weighted average. More specifically, it is given by:

$$w_1 sim(L_i, L_j) + w_2 sim(N_i, N_j) + w_3 sim(I_i, I_j) + w_4 sim(VT_i, VT_j) , \tag{4.2}$$

where w_1, w_2, w_3 and $w_4 > 0$ and their sum is 1.

The computation of similarity between two labels is as follows. Each label is represented by a set of terms, after stop words are removed and the content words are stemmed. Each set of content words in a label forms a vector, where each dimension represents a stemmed content word. A component of a vector is the number of occurrences (usually 1) of the corresponding stemmed word. A similarity function such as the *Cosine* function [Salton and McGill, 1983], can then be used to compute the similarity. In case some terms in one label are synonymous with some terms in the other label, WordNet [Fellbaum, 1998] can be utilized to perform the match. Since a word can have quite a few synonyms, only the synonyms in the first two dominant synsets (determined by WordNet) are used.

An internal name is usually a single word. The similarity function between two internal names can be an inverse function of the *edit distance* of the two strings representing the two internal names. The edit distance of two strings is the number of edit operations (deletion, insertion, and replacement) that need to be performed to convert one string to the other string. One possible similarity function is $1 - \frac{edit(N_i, N_j)}{\max(|N_i|, |N_j|)}$. If the two internal names are identical, then their edit distance is 0 and the similarity will be 1; in the other extreme, if the two strings have no character in common, then the edit distance is the length of longer of the two strings and the similarity will be 0. Another similarity function can be the normalized common substring in which the length of the longest common substring between the two strings is obtained and is then divided by the length of the longer string.

The computation of the similarity between two value types is simple. Given two value types VT_i and VT_j, their similarity is 1 if they are identical else it is 0. The value types such as integer, text, and floating points can be recognized. It is also possible to recognize other types such as day, month, and year.

For the computation of the similarity between two sets of instances I_i and I_j, consider the two cases: (i) each instance is a set of words, and (ii) each instance is a numerical value. In case (i), the similarity, say using the *Cosine* function, is computed between every pair of instances, with one instance of a pair from I_i and the other instance of the pair from I_j. Take the pair, say (v_i, v_j), with the highest similarity. If it is higher than or equal to a threshold (which indicates that they are sufficiently similar), then delete the instance v_i from I_i and the corresponding instance, v_j from I_j. The assumption is that each instance of I_i should be similar to at most one instance of I_j, so if v_i is most similar to v_j, then no other instance from I_j should match v_i and no other instance from I_i should match v_j. This resembles the "best marriage" situation in which each person selects one and only one spouse provided that the selection criterion, namely the threshold, is satisfied. It is important that exact match is not required, as two instances may be somewhat different but refer to the same concept. For example, one instance can be "New York," while the corresponding instance can be "New York City." After all the matching pairs are determined, let the number of such pairs be k. Then, the similarity between I_i and I_j is $k/(|I_i| + |I_j|)$.

The computation of the similarity between I_i and I_j when they contain numerical values is somewhat different from that given above. Suppose I_i and I_j contain prices of real estate. It is possible that no two prices are identical. In this case, the similarity can be defined as the range of values that overlap between I_i and I_j divided by the range from the lowest value of the two domains to the highest value of the two domains. Specifically, the similarity is defined as

$$\frac{\min\left\{\max\{I_i\}, \max\{I_j\}\right\} - \max\left\{\min\{I_i\}, \min\{I_j\}\right\}}{\max\left\{\max\{I_i\}, \max\{I_j\}\right\} - \min\left\{\min\{I_i\}, \min\{I_j\}\right\}} , \tag{4.3}$$

where $\max\{I_i\}$ and $\min\{I_i\}$ are the maximum value and the minimum value of I_i, respectively.

As pointed out above, the similarity between one component (such as label) of one attribute and the same component of another attribute can be obtained by various similarity functions. Thus, it is possible to combine similarity values computed by different similarity functions (called *ensemble matcher* in Gal [2011]) into a single one. One popular combination function is a weighted average of the similarity values. The ensemble approach is also applicable to pairs of attributes instead of pairs of components of attributes.

In Formula (4.2), usually $w_1 \geq w_2$, because the internal names can be rather obscure; $w_3 \geq w_4$, because instance match carries more positive information than value type match. In fact, if the value types of the two attributes are different, their value type similarity and their instance similarity are 0. (Note that it is possible that in one query interface, month is written in character form such as January and in a different user interface, it is an integer from 1 to 12. In that case, unless domain knowledge is applied, the value type similarity and the instance similarity are 0.) When training examples are available, these weights w_1, w_2, w_3, and w_4 can be learned.

When the similarities between pairs of attributes in multiple query interfaces have been computed, we need to identify which attributes in one query interface are equivalent to which attributes in the other interfaces. We first consider the case where the attribute equivalence is 1:1. Another possibility is 1:m, in which one attribute in one interface is equivalent to m attributes in the other interface. It will be discussed immediately after the 1:1 case.

A strategy to find equivalent attributes across multiple user interfaces depends on two observations.

Observation 1. It may be difficult to find the equivalence between two attributes, if the number of query interfaces is restricted to 2. But, as the number of query interfaces on the same application domain increases, the determination of equivalence of attributes becomes easier due to the *bridging effect*. As an example, consider two attributes from the user interfaces shown in Figure 4.1, the attribute A with the label *Depart City* and no instance, and the attribute B with the label *Leaving from* and no instance. In this example, no internal name is used, for the sake of simplicity. Since no instance is given, no similarity between instances is obtained. (Since no instance is given, it can be assumed that the value types of the attributes are *text*. Although the types are the same, since w_4 is small the equivalence between A and B cannot be established.) The labels of the two attributes are all distinct. If no electronic dictionary such as WordNet is used, then the similarity between the two attributes on label is zero. Even if WordNet is used and "depart" is found to be a synonym of "leave," the similarity may not be large enough for the attributes to be determined to be equivalent. However, if the interface in Figure 4.3 is also utilized, the attribute C with the label "Departing from" and no instance can be utilized to improve the matching. It is clear that the attribute A and attribute C have the word "depart" in common after stemming is applied. They can be determined to be equivalent. Similarly, attribute B and attribute C can be determined to have the word "from" in common and can be equivalent. Since equivalence is a transitive relation, attribute A and attribute B are equivalent. In terms of computation, we assume that $sim(A, B) = min\{sim(A, C), sim(B, C)\}$.

The underlying basic principle of establishing equivalence among attributes in the above example is that there are very few words that are suitable in describing an attribute. Thus, if we consider a reasonably large number of query interfaces, each having that attribute or its equivalence, then the words in describing it will repeat in multiple query interfaces [He and Chang, 2003] (Section 2.1.2), as shown in the above example. Based on the above argument, it is easier to establish attribute equivalence when a substantial number of query interfaces are considered than when only two query interfaces are examined. Thus, as many query interfaces in the same application domain should be used for query interface integration.

Observation 2. The "best marriage" principle which applies to matching instances in two attributes also applies to the determination of equivalent attributes. Specifically, each 1:1 match between two query interfaces should match one attribute in one query interface with at most one attribute in the other interface.

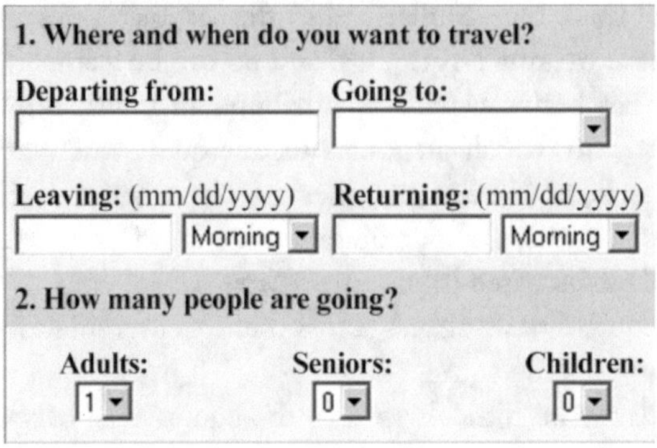

Figure 4.3: A query interface in the airfare domain.

Suppose an attribute A in query interface QI_1 matches an attribute B in query interface QI_2. Then A will not match any other attribute in QI_2 nor will attribute B match any other attribute in QI_1. Thus, whenever two attributes, A and B, from two query interfaces are determined to be equivalent, all similarities of the form $sim(A, x)$ and $sim(y, B)$ should be removed, where x and y are attributes of the interfaces QI_1 and QI_2, respectively. The removal occurs before the next pair of attributes from the two query interfaces is considered for equivalence. The starting point is to have the largest similarity between any two attributes from any two query interfaces and to consider the pair having this largest value to be equivalent, provided that the similarity exceeds a reasonable threshold.

4.3.2   1:M MATCHING

We now discuss 1:m matchings. There are two different types of 1:m matchings: *aggregate* and *IS-A* matchings. For the first type, a set of attributes $\{A_1, A_2, .., A_m\}$ in one query interface can be aggregated to form a composite attribute B in another query interface. Each attribute A_i can be considered as a part of attribute B. As an example, in one query interface the name of a person is modeled as a single attribute "full name," while in a different user interface, there are two attributes "first name" and "last name." It is obvious that the aggregation of the latter two attributes is equivalent to the composite attribute "full name."

For the second type of 1:m matching, a value of an attribute on the many-side of the *IS-A* relationship is an instance of the attribute on the 1-side. For example, consider the composite attribute *Passengers* with sub-attributes *Adult* and *Child* and the single attribute *Passengers* (as shown in Figure 4.1). Each adult passenger is a passenger; each child passenger is also a passenger. The key heuristics to identify 1:m matches are as follows:

1. The m attributes are close together in the query interface. For instance, in the example involving the aggregate attributes, "first name" and "last name" are close together; similarly, in the example involving the *IS-A* relationship, *Adult* and *Child* are close by (see Figure 4.1).

2. Corresponding labels have significant similarities. In the example involving the name attributes, "full name" has high similarities with "first name" and with "last name." In the example involving passengers (see Figure 4.1), the parent attribute of *Adult* and *Child* in one of the query interfaces is *Passengers* (or a synonym such as traveler), which is identical to the attribute label *Passengers* in the other query interface.

3. Usually, there are some similarities between the value type of an attribute in one query interface with the value type of the corresponding attribute in a different query interface. In the name example, the value types are both character string although instances are usually not shown in the query interface. In the passengers example, the value types are integer; some instances are shown (see Figure 4.1) and can be found to have quite a few identical entries. If instances are shown for the aggregate attributes in the query interfaces, then on the 1 side, each instance is a concatenation of the entries of the corresponding attributes on the m side. For example, an instance of *Departure Date* can be May 2011, while in a different query interface the same instance can be represented by the instance "May" in the attribute *Month* and the instance "2011" in the attribute *Year*. In practice, all the months from January to December are shown in the latter query interface; as are the years from 2011 to 2012. (In the flight reservation application, a reservation is usually no more than one year away). Thus, an instance of an attribute in the former query interface can be obtained by concatenating an instance of an attribute with that of another attribute in the latter query interface.

Other heuristics may be employed to recognize 1:m relationships that are not recognizable by the above heuristics [Wu et al., 2004].

Sometimes, it may not be possible to find directly a 1:m match across two query interfaces. As an example, in one query interface, QI_1, there is a composite (aggregate) attribute *Choose a vehicle* in which instances such as "Toyota-Camry" are given and in a different query interface, QI_2, there are two attributes, *Model* and *Brand*, where *Model* has no instances, but *Brand* has instances such as "Toyota." It is difficult to match *Choose a vehicle* to *Model* and *Brand*, due to the low similarity between their terms as well as between the instances of the composite attribute in QI_1 and those of the two attributes in QI_2. However, in the presence of a third user interface, QI_3, which has two attributes *Make* with instances such as "Toyota" and *Model* with instances such as "Camry," the matching between the composite attribute in QI_1 and the two attributes in QI_2 is possible via the interface QI_3. Specifically, many instances in *Choose a vehicle* can be composed from instances of *Make* concatenated with instances of *Model*. Furthermore, the attribute *Model* in QI_3 matches the same label in QI_2; the attribute *Make* matches (to some extent) with the attribute *Brand* by WordNet and the instances in *Make* matches those in *Brand*. Thus, if there is a 1:m match between a composite attribute C in query interface QI_1 and a set X_3 of simple attributes in another query interface QI_3 and there is a 1:1 match between each attribute in the set of attributes in QI_3 and each attribute in the set of attributes X_2 in query interface QI_2, then there is a 1:m match between C in QI_1 and the set of attributes X_2 in QI_2.

In summary, the matching of attributes across different query interfaces is as follows. Perform initial 1:m matching, based on a set of heuristics, some are identified in steps (a)–(c). Perform 1:1 matching, using the "best marriage" principle. Deduce additional 1:m matching, using the results of the last two steps.

4.3.3   CLUSTERING BY POSITIVE AND PREDICTIVE MATCHES

In this approach, query interfaces are *flat*, i.e., each consisting of a set of attributes. This method performs two tasks: one is to find the matching attributes from query interfaces to be integrated, and the other is to determine what global attribute name should be used for each group of matching attributes. The latter task is described in Section 5.2.1. It classifies matches into two types: *positive matches* and *predictive matches*. *Positive matches* include exact label match, semantic (synonymy, hypernymy, and meronymy) matches and value-based match (i.e., instance-based matches). For value-based match, it employs exact match, approximate string match, synonymy match, and hypernymy match to compare values. When *enough* values from the two attributes are matched (a threshold is used), value-based match is recognized as successful. When one of the positive matches occurs, the corresponding attributes are recognized as matched. *Predictive matches* consist of approximate name match, vector space similarity match of labels, and matches based on scale, domain type, value type, default value, *Boolean* property, and value pattern. Predictive matches must be sufficiently strong (based on a weight threshold) for two attributes to be recognized as matched.

Clustering by Positive Matches

This is to group attributes into clusters based on the positive matches between attributes. This phase considers all interfaces. There are three steps for the clustering:

Group attributes into clusters based on the exact match of attribute labels in all interfaces of the same domain. After this step, all attributes in the same cluster have the same attribute label. Values of all attributes in each cluster, if any, are merged by performing a union.

Merge the clusters produced in the first step based on the matching of values in each cluster and the semantic (synonymy, hypernymy, and meronymy) matches of attribute labels. New clusters are generated in this step.

Determine the *representative attribute label* for all attributes in each cluster produced in the second step. Generally, the representative attribute label of each cluster is selected using the *majority rule:* choose the attribute label that appears in most interfaces in a cluster. The semantic relationships among attribute labels in a cluster are also employed to find a representative label that is more general. For example, if a cluster contains two different attribute labels *Title* and

Book Title, then *Title* is chosen as the representative label even if *Book Title* appears in more interfaces because *Title* is a hypernym of *Book Title* (see Section 5.2.1 for details).

At the end of the above steps, each attribute A belongs to a cluster and has a corresponding representative attribute label, denoted by $RL(A)$. While positive matches generally ensure that attributes in the same cluster are correctly matched, they may still leave some attributes not clustered with their matching attributes due to the lack of required positive matches. The next phase tries to remedy this problem by utilizing predictive matches. The clusters generated above are not used in the next phase directly but the knowledge derived from these clusters, namely there is an $RL(A)$ for each attribute A, will be used.

Clustering by Predictive Matches

The method for this clustering starts with a single local interface and forms singleton clusters based on each attribute in the interface. Let $C = \{C_1, ..., C_k\}$ denote these cluster. For each remaining local interface QI, the method tries to place each attribute in QI into one of the existing clusters, and if this fails, it forms a new cluster based on this attribute. Let A be an attribute in QI. The following three cases are considered.

1. An attribute with the same label as A is already in one of the clusters, say C^*, in C. In this case, just add A to C^*.

2. The label of A is different from all the labels of the attributes already in existing clusters but $RL(A)$ is the same as the label of one of the attributes in a cluster C^* in C. In this case, add A to C^*.

3. None of the above cases is true. In this case, compute a *matching weight* between A and each existing cluster C_i, $mw(A, C_i)$, $i = 1, ..., k$, where $mw(A, C_i)$ is defined as the average of the *matching weight* between A and every attribute in C_i. Let C^* be the cluster in C that has the largest matching weight with A. If $mw(A, C^*) > \tau$, where τ is an empirically set threshold, then add A to C^*. Otherwise, create a new cluster using A and add the cluster to C.

The above process is repeated for each attribute in QI and for each remaining local query interface. After all query interfaces are processed, each cluster in C represents one set of matching attributes across different query interfaces.

We now describe the method for computing the matching weight between two attributes A and B. This weight is computed using the following eight metrics [He et al., 2003]:

1. *Approximate sting match.* If the edit-distance between the labels of A and B is within the allowed threshold T, assign a positive weight W_{am}; otherwise W_{am} is 0.

2. *Vector space similarity.* The weight of this metric is the *Cosine* similarity of the labels of A and B.

3. *Compatible domain.* Four domain types are considered: *finite*, *infinite*, *hybrid*, and *range*. *Hybrid* is the combination of finite and infinite. If an attribute domain is *hybrid*, users can either select from a list of pre-compiled values or fill in a new value. *Hybrid* is compatible with *finite* and *infinite*; the same types are compatible. If two attributes have compatible domain types, assign a weight W_{cd}; otherwise W_{cd} is 0. If two attributes have range domain type, double W_{cd}.

4. *Value type match.* Six value types are considered: date, time, currency, number, char, and id. If two attributes have the same value type, assign a weight W_{vtm}; otherwise $W_{vtm} = 0$.

5. *Scale/unit match.* Consider two attributes that have the same value type. If they also have the same scale or unit, assign a weight W_{cs}. If they have different value types or different scales/units, W_{cs} is 0. For example, if two attributes are both of currency type and their values are in US\$, then W_{cs} is assigned to the overall match of the two attributes.

6. *Default value.* Some attributes may have default values. This is particularly useful for textboxes. If an attribute is in a cluster, then its default value is considered as one of the default values of the cluster. If two attributes have the same default value, assign a weight W_{dv}; otherwise $W_{dv} = 0$.

7. *Boolean property.* If an attribute has just a single checkbox then it is considered to have a Boolean property. If both attributes have the Boolean property, assign a weight W_{bp}; otherwise $W_{bp} = 0$.

8. *Value pattern.* It is applied only to numeric attributes. The average of all numerical values in each attribute is computed. If the two averages are close, assign a weight W_{vp}; otherwise $W_{vp} = 0$.

Finally, $mw(A, B)$ is computed as the sum of the above eight weights. The values of these weights are determined experimentally [He et al., 2003].

4.4   STATISTICAL-BASED ATTRIBUTE MATCHING

The statistical schema matching approach is motivated by the observation that while the number of Web databases increases on the Web, they exhibit useful regularities. For instance, the *schema vocabulary* of the sources within an application domain tends to converge (at a relatively small size) [He and Chang, 2003]. For example, for the sources in the book domain two key observations are drawn: (1) 92% of their attributes are observed at 25th source and 98% at 35th and (2) they share 12 frequent attributes, which account for 78% of all attribute occurrences. In general, in an application domain, if we take the frequency of an attribute to be the number of query interfaces in which the attribute occurs and order the frequencies over their ranks, then a Zipf-like distribution for the frequencies of the attributes can be observed (Section 2.1.2). Statistical-based approaches attempt to capitalize on the emergence of patterns among attributes in a domain as large sets of query interfaces are analyzed. In this subsection, we present two representative statistical approaches: *statistical model discovery* [He and Chang, 2003] and *correlation mining* [He et al., 2004a; Nguyen et al., 2010;

Su et al., 2006a]. The former hypothesizes that in a domain there exists a hidden generative random process, called *hidden schema model,* with a specific distribution that describes how schemas in the domain are generated from a finite vocabulary of attribute labels. The statistical problem is that of reconstructing the hidden generative distribution from a set of input schemas (training set). The MGS_{sd} algorithm [He and Chang, 2003] aims to realize this statistical approach for query interface matching. We describe it next.

4.4.1 MGS_{sd} ALGORITHM FOR SCHEMA MATCHING

This approach finds only 1:1 matches and views a query interface as a flat schema, i.e., a set of attributes. The query interface-matching problem is pursued as a *synonym discovery* problem. Across different interfaces, some attributes are synonyms for the same concepts. For example, the attributes "author" and "name," or "subject" and "category," are synonyms for the "author" and "subject" concepts respectively, in the book domain. The query interface-matching problem then becomes that of finding the synonyms among the input attributes. The MGS_{sd} algorithm has three steps: *hypothesis modeling*, *hypothesis generation*, and *hypothesis selection*. They are described one by one below.

Hypothesis Modeling

The construction of the generative model is governed by the following assumptions:

1. *Concept mutual-independence.* A query interface contains several different concepts (e.g., "author" or "subject"). We assume that, when generating a query interface different concepts are selected independently.

2. *Synonym mutual-exclusion.* This assumption assumes that in generating an interface schema, no two synonyms will be selected when multiple synonyms exist for a concept. The presence of synonyms in a query interface would create redundancy and confusion. An analysis of several hundreds of interfaces shows that this assumption holds in practice [He and Chang, 2003].

3. *Non-overlapping concepts.* Here it is assumed that no distinct concepts share attributes. This assumption essentially says that there is an "inherent" partition over the vocabulary of a domain so that synonymous attribute belong to the same subset in the partition. For instance, the concepts {"author," "name"} and {"subject," "category"} do not overlap. There are instances when this assumption is violated in practice. For example, in the real estate domain, the following two distinct concepts {"area," "minimum floor area"} and {"area," "location"} have an overlapping attribute "area."

These assumptions shape the structure of the hidden schema model. Namely, all attributes in a domain are partitioned into concepts and each concept consists of synonymous attributes. The model then generates schemas by first independently selecting a concept according to a probability distribution and, from a selected concept, the model selects one of its member attributes with another probability distribution. Formally, the schema model is a 4-tuple $M = (V, C, P_c, P_a)$, where V is the vocabulary of attribute labels, C is the *concept partition* that partitions V, P_c is the probability distribution over the concepts C and P_a is the probability function for attributes. For every concept C_i in C, $\sum\limits_{A \in C_i} P_a(A) = 1$, where A is an attribute in C_i.

Example 4.1   Figure 4.4 depicts an example of a schema model M_B in the book domain. A model is represented by parenthesizing attributes in concepts with probability annotations. $M_B = \{(author : \beta_1, name : \beta_2) : \alpha_1, (title : \beta_3) : \alpha_2, (ISBN : \beta4) : \alpha_3, (subject : \beta_5, category : \beta_6) : \alpha_4\}$, $V = \{author, name, title, ISBN, subject, category\}$ and $C = \{C_1, C_2, C_3, C_4\}$.

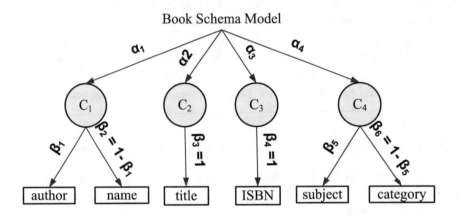

Figure 4.4: An example of schema model in the book domain.

We now describe how a schema model M generates interface schemas. A concept $C_i \in C$ appears in an interface with probability $\Pr(C_i|M) = \alpha_i$ or otherwise $\Pr(\neg C_i|M) = 1 - \alpha_i$. An attribute $A_j \in V$ is selected from M with the probability

$$\Pr(A_j|M) = \begin{cases} \alpha_i \beta_j, & \exists i : A_j \in C_i \\ 0, & \text{otherwise} \end{cases}.$$

A set of attributes $\{A_1, \ldots, A_m\}$ is selected from M with the following probability:

$$\Pr(A_1, \ldots, A_m|M) = \begin{cases} 0, & \exists j \neq k, \exists i : A_j \in C_i \wedge A_k \in C_i \\ \prod\limits_{j=1}^{m} \Pr(A_j|M), & \text{otherwise} \end{cases}.$$

Let $\Pr(S|M)$ denote the probability that M generates an interface schema $S = \{A_1, \ldots, A_m\}$. This is the probability of used attributes times the probability of unselected concepts in S:

$$\Pr(S|M) = \Pr(A_1, \ldots, A_m|M) \times \prod\limits_{\forall A_j, A_j \notin C_i} \Pr(\neg C_i|M). \tag{4.4}$$

The schema model M generates schema S if $Pr(S|M) > 0$.

Example 4.2   Consider two schemas $S_1 = \{title, category, ISBN\}$ and $S_2 = \{author, name, ISBN, subject\}$ and the generative model in Figure 4.4. We have

$$Pr(S_1|M) = (1 - \alpha_1) \times (\alpha_2 \times \beta_3) \times (\alpha_3 \times \beta_4) \times (\alpha_4 \times \beta_6)$$
$$= (1 - \alpha_1)^2 \times \alpha_2 \times \alpha_3 \times \alpha_4 \times \beta_6 ,$$

and $Pr(S_2|M) = 0$ since *author* and *name* both belong to C_1.

The goal now is to build a schema model M from a set of input schemas Ω, which serve as observations. Note that a schema may appear multiple times among the observations because many query interfaces on the Web share the same schema. Among all the hidden models, those models M that generate all schemas in Ω are needed. In other words, we want the models that satisfy $Pr(\Omega|M) = \prod_{S_i \in \Omega} Pr(S_i|M)^{b_i} > 0$, where b_i is the occurrence count of schema S_i in Ω. Such a model is called *consistent*. The hypothesis generation, which is covered next, finds these consistent models as candidate hidden models.

Hypothesis Generation
Recall that a model is a 4-tuple $M = (V, C, P_c, P_a)$. So, to generate a candidate model M, we need to determine each of the four components of M. First, we determine V from the schemas in Ω, namely $V = \bigcup_{S \in \Omega} S$. Second, we need to determine C, which is a partition over V. This task is difficult because in general a large number of partitions are possible for a set. One way to address this problem is to eliminate as many partitions that satisfy $Pr(\Omega|M) = 0$ as possible. The following property helps identify many such models.

Let $C = \{C_1, \ldots, C_m\}$ be a concept partition for V. Any model constructed from C has $Pr(\Omega|M) = 0$ if for some attributes A_i and A_k, both of the following conditions hold: (1) $\exists S \in \Omega$, such that $A_i, A_k \in S$ and (2) $\exists C_i \in C$, such that $A_i, A_k \in C_i$.

A concept C_i that does not contain a pair of attributes with the above property is called *consistent*. Using this property, we can look for the models whose concept partitions do not satisfy this property. This can be accomplished as follows. First, a co-occurrence graph, called *concept network*, of the attributes in V is constructed. In the graph, a node represents an attribute and there is an edge between two attributes if and only if they do not occur together in any of the schemas in Ω. Next, all cliques in this graph are identified. A clique represents a consistent concept because it is a set of non-co-occurring attributes. From the set of consistent concepts so generated, a partition of V can be constructed by selecting a subset of them with the property that they are disjoint and cover V. The latter property is needed because of the non-overlapping concepts assumption. This corresponds to a variation of the *set covering problem*.

Example 4.3   Suppose that $\Omega = \{S_1, S_2\}$, where the two schemas S_1 and S_2 are shown in Figure 4.5. We build their concept network. For example, *author* and *title* do not have an edge because they co-occur in S_2, whereas *author* and *category* have an edge since they do not co-occur in any schema. There are 7 cliques: {*author*}, {*title*}, {*subject*}, {*category*}, {*ISBN*}, {*category author*}, and {*subject, category*}. We can construct three consistent models $M_1 = \{(author), (title), (ISBN), (subject), (category)\}$; $M_2 = \{(author), (title), (ISBN), (subject, category)\}$; $M_3 = \{(author, category), (title), (ISBN), (subject)\}$. Hence, the hypothesis space is $\{M_1, M_2, M_3\}$.

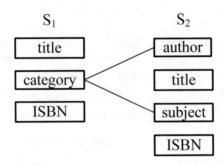

Figure 4.5: An example of a concept network.

We also have to determine P_c and P_a for each model. They are given by:

$$\max_{P_c, P_a} \Pr(\Omega, M(V, C, P_c, P_a)) .$$

(4.5)

This corresponds to the *maximum likelihood estimation* problem [Casella and Berger, 2001] for given V and C. Formula (4.5) has the solutions:

$$\alpha_i^* = \frac{\sum\limits_{A_j \in C_i} O_j}{|\Omega|}, \qquad \beta_j^* = \frac{O_j}{\sum\limits_{A_j \in C_i} O_j},$$

where O_j is the frequency of occurrence of the attribute A_j in Ω, and $|\Omega|$ is the number of observed schemas.

Hypothesis Selection

From the set of all generated hypothesis (models), the ones that are sufficiently consistent with the observed schemas need to be selected. χ^2 hypothesis testing [Casella and Berger, 2001] is used to measure how consistent a schema model is with the data.

Because the vocabulary of attributes in a domain follows a Zipf-like distribution, MGS_{sd} requires some adjustments to cope with the attributes on either end of the Zipf distribution (i.e., the very frequent and rare attributes) [He and Chang, 2003].

The time complexity of the algorithm is exponential in the number of attributes. However, this is acceptable in practice because interface schema matching is performed off-line and in many practical cases the running time of the algorithm is within a minute [He and Chang, 2003].

4.4.2   CORRELATION MINING

Most schema matching techniques address 1:1 matching. However, among query interfaces complex matchings do exist and are quite frequent. For instance, in airfare domain, as Figure 4.1 illustrates, we have the 1:2 matching between *Passengers* and {*Adult, Child*}. As another example, in books domain, *Author* matches the attributes *Last Name* and *First Name*, i.e., {*Author*} = {*First Name, Last Name*}. Hence, discovering complex matchings is critical in the task of integrating query interfaces of Web databases. In general, complex matching relates a set of *m* attributes in one interface to a set of *n* attributes in another interface, which is also called *m:n matching*. The analysis of the *co-occurrence patterns* of attributes across query interface proves to be an effective method for discovering complex matchings [He et al., 2004a; Su et al., 2006a]. These two techniques are very similar in spirit and find complex matchings using a *correlation mining* approach. In this subsection, we mainly present the method by He et al. [2004a].

In Chapter 2, we discussed about attributes being grouped together to form larger concepts or *attribute groups* (e.g., *Adult, Child*, and *Senior* form such a group in the interface in Figure 2.1.). We use the set notation to denote attribute groups. Attribute groups in a matching are referred to as *synonym groups*. The first key observation of this technique is that attributes in such a group often co-occur across query interfaces and, thus, they are *positively correlated*. The second key observation is that an attribute group rarely co-occurs in query interfaces with its matches, i.e., they are *negatively correlated*. For example, *Adult, Senior, Child*, and *Infant* often co-occur with each other in query interfaces, while they together do not co-occur often with *Passenger*.

With the above observations, the query interface matching problem becomes: Given a set of schemas $S = \{S_1, S_2, ..., S_n\}$ in the same application domain, identify all the matches $M = \{m_1, ..., m_v\}$ where each m_j represents a complex matching $G_{j_1} = G_{j_2} = \ldots = G_{j_w}$, with each G_{j_k} being a positively correlated attribute group and $G_{j_k} \subseteq \bigcup_{i=1}^{n} S_i$. Semantically, each m_j represents the synonym relationship of attribute groups $G_{j_1}, G_{j_2}, \ldots, G_{j_w}$. Each schema S_i is considered as a transaction of attributes.

An example of a matching m_j is {*Adult, Child, Infant, Senior*} = {*Passengers*} = {*Number of Passengers*}.

The matching algorithm we describe here has three steps: *group discovery, matching discovery*, and *matching selection*.

Group Discovery

This step mines co-occurring attributes. It is developed in the spirit of the classic apriori algorithm for association rule mining. From the set of input interfaces *S*, it first finds the set of all attribute groups of size two, denoted by X_2, that are positively correlated. Then the algorithm uses X_2 to find the set of all attribute groups of size 3. And, it continues as long as the *apriori condition* can be satisfied. That is, if X_l is the set of all attribute groups of size l, then a group $g \in X_l$ if every subgroup of g of size $(l-1)$ is in X_{l-1}. The algorithm uses the following correlation measure. Two attributes A and B are correlated if $cm_+(A, B) > \tau_+$, where cm_+ is a positive correlation measure, which will be defined shortly, and τ_+ is a given threshold. A set of attributes $\{A_1, \ldots, A_n\}$ is positively correlated if:

$$C_{\min}(\{A_1, \ldots, A_n\}) = \min_{i \neq j} cm_+(A_i, A_j) > \tau_+ . \tag{4.6}$$

Matching Discovery
This step is to find the attribute groups, determined in the previous step, that are negatively correlated. Since 1:1 and 1:*m* are particular instances of the $m : n$ matchings, groups with one attribute need to be considered in this step. The procedure is very similar to the previous one. There are two distinctions between them. In this step, we need (1) a different measure to determine negatively correlated attributes and (2) the input schemas to be changed to reflect the positively correlated attribute groups.

A set of attribute groups $\{G_1, \ldots, G_m\}$ is negatively correlated attribute groups if

$$C_{\min}(\{G_1, \ldots, G_m\}) = \min_{i \neq j} cm_-(G_i, G_j) > \tau_- , \tag{4.7}$$

where cm_- is a measure for negative correlation and τ_- is a given threshold.

Each schema $S_i \in S$ is modified so that it becomes a set of positively correlated attribute groups. Let G be the set of positively correlated attribute groups. For each $g \in G$ such that $g \cap S_i \neq \emptyset$, $S_i = S_i \cup \{g\}$. For example, if $g = \{First Name, Last Name\}$ and S_i has only *Last Name*, then *Last Name* is replaced by g in S_i. Hence, for the purpose of mining negatively correlated groups, each schema is now a transaction of groups.

Matching Selection
The matching discovery step may produce wrong matchings along with the correct ones. The goal of this step is to sort out the correct from the wrong matchings. This is accomplished by *ranking* the discovered matchings and by eliminating the *conflicting matchings*. We present the ranking part first. For a matching $m_j = \{G_{j_1}, G_{j_2}, \ldots, G_{j_w}\}$, let u_j be the vector of the top-k cm_- values among the pairs of groups in m_j. That is, $u_j[1] = \max cm_-(G_{j_r}, G_{j_t}), \forall j_r \neq j_t, j_r, j_t \in [j_1, j_w], u_j[2]$ is the second highest cm_-, and so on. Between two matchings m_j and m_i, m_j is ranked higher than m_i if $(\exists r, 1 \leq r \leq k)(\forall t < r)(u_i[t] = u_j[t]) \wedge (u_i[r] < u_j[r])$. If u_j and u_j are equal, then a tie breaker is needed. We say that m_j *semantically subsumes* m_i, denoted $m_i \prec m_j$, if all the semantic relationships in m_i are covered in m_j. For example, $\{Passengers\} = \{Adult, Child\} \prec \{Passengers\} = \{Adult, Child, Infant, Senior\}$ because the synonym relationship in the first matching is part of the second. The relationship serves as the tie breaker, i.e., if u_j and u_j are equal then m_j is ranked higher than m_i if $m_i \prec m_j$. Otherwise, m_j and m_i are ranked randomly.

Consider the matchings {*Passengers*} = {*Adult, Child, Infant, Senior*} and {*Number of Stops*} = {*Adult, Child, Infant, Senior*}. Due to the transitivity of synonym relationship, we get {*Passengers*} = {*Number of Stops*}, which is wrong. Therefore, the above two matches cannot both be correct. This is called a *matching conflict*.

The matching selection algorithm is a greedy algorithm that in each iteration selects the highest ranked matching and removes inconsistent parts from the remaining matchings.

Example 4.4   Consider the following matchings along with their score in the airfare domain:

m_1 = {*Passengers*} = {*Adult, Child, Infant, Senior*}, 0.95
m_2 = {*Passengers*} = {*Adult, Child, Senior*}, 0.95
m_3 = {*Connections*} = {*Number of Stops*}, 0.92
m_4 = {*Number of Stops*} = {*Adult, Child*}, 0.90
m_5 = {*Number of Stops*} = {*Adult, Child, Infant, Senior*}, 0.88

In the first iteration, we select m_1. Note that although m_1 and m_2 have the same score, $m_1 \prec m_2$, thus m_1 is ranked ahead of m_2. We now remove the conflicting parts from the rest of the matchings. {*Passengers*} is removed from m_2 and {*Adult, Child, Infant, Senior*} is removed from m_5. Both m_5 and m_2 are discarded because they do not represent matches anymore. Next we select m_3. We remove {*Number of Stops*} from m_4 and m_4 is discarded. The selection algorithm terminates because there are no more candidate matches. So, the output is m_1 and m_3.

	A_p	$\neg A_p$	
A_q	f_{11}	f_{10}	f_{1+}
$\neg A_q$	f_{01}	f_{00}	f_{0+}
	f_{+1}	f_{+0}	f_{++}

Table 4.1: Contingency Table for a Test of Correlation

Correlation Measure

We briefly discussed here the choice for the positive measure cm_+ and the negative measure cm_-. There are many correlation measures in statistics, e.g., *lift* and χ^2. However, due to the peculiarity of query interfaces (e.g., Zipf-like distribution of the attributes), it was found that these measures were not adequate for this application. cm_- and cm_+ are defined as follows. Let A_p and A_q be two attributes and let the Table 4.2 be their contingency table. In the table, f_{11} is the co-presence count of A_p and A_q, f_{10} and f_{01} are the cross-presence counts of A_p and A_q, and f_{00} is the co-absent count of A_p and A_q. The negative correlation is defined as:

$$cm_-(A_p, A_q) = \frac{f_{01} f_{10}}{f_{+1} f_{1+}} \, ,$$

and the positive correlation is defined as:

$$cm_+(A_p, A_q) = \begin{cases} 1 - cm_-(A_p, A_q), & \text{if } \frac{f_{11}}{f_{++}} < \tau_d \\ 0, & \text{otherwise} \end{cases} ,$$

where τ_d is a threshold to filter out false grouping.

The matching algorithm HSM by Su et al. [2006a] distinguishes from the above method in two key ways. First, it uses a different measure for negative correlation:

$$X_{pq} = \begin{cases} 0, & \text{if } (A_p, A_q) \notin L \\ \frac{(f_{+1} - f_{11})(f_{1+} - f_{11})}{f_{+1} + f_{1+}}, & \text{otherwise} \end{cases} ,$$

where L is the set of candidate pairs of synonym attributes. Second, HSM discovers matches faster. Its time complexity is polynomial in the number of attributes, while the time complexity of the algorithm by He et al. [2004a] is exponential. The reason is that HSM only considers the grouping scores between pairs of attributes, and the complex matching is discovered by adding each newly found group member into the corresponding group incrementally.

4.5   INSTANCE BASED ATTRIBUTE MATCHING

The performance of query interface matching is in general affected when no attribute description is available or the identified description is not informative, as well as when attributes lack instances. Motivated by these shortcomings a couple of works [Wang et al., 2004; Wu et al., 2006a] explore matching techniques that primarily use instances acquired from the Web. Instances can be gathered from the result pages of deep Web sources [Wang et al., 2004] and from the Web at large [Wu et al., 2006a]. This section primarily covers the former technique.

4.5.1   MATCHING BY QUERY PROBING

This query interface matching method discovers only 1:1 matches and starts from the following assumptions:

1. *Query submission. Proper queries* return result pages with many records and the query keywords appear very frequently in the corresponding attributes of the records. *Improper queries* return result pages with very few or no result records. A *proper query* formulated on a query interface is a query that correctly matches the query keywords and the input fields of the query interface.

2. *Global schema.* For each application domain (e.g., real estate), there exists a *global schema* GS that represents the key attributes of the domain.

3. *Instances.* The global schema has a sample of data instances.

The last two assumptions are needed in order to formulate probing queries. The global schema along with its instances is manually defined.

In general, the schema of the Web database is not available. However, two other schemas can be extracted from the front-end of the deep Web site: the *interface schema* (IS) and *result schema* (RS). The former is the set of attributes of the query interface, while the latter consists of data attributes that users can browse. This technique aims to automatically discover the matches between semantically related attributes of ISs and RSs from multiple Web databases (i.e., *inter-site schema matching*) as well as the matches between the IS and RS of a Web database. The matching of RSs is also studied by Chuang and Chang [2008]. We use Figure 4.6, which shows a bookstore website, to illustrate these concepts. The figure shows the outcome of a proper query submission: *Title =* "Narnia" and the rest of the attributes having default values. The website returns many results pages for this query. Figure 4.6 depicts the global schema (center), the query interface (on the left), and the result page (on the right). The various lines in the figure show the semantic correspondences between the three schemas. The dotted lines show the correspondence between the attributes of the GS and IS. The solid lines relate the attributes of the IS and the instance values in the result page. Finally, the dashed lines relate the attributes of the GS and the instance values in the result page. Note that if we submit an improper query, say *ISBN =* "Narnia," no result would be returned.

Query Probing

Queries are formulated such that only the value of one of the fields is varied while the values for the rest of the fields of a query interface use the default. The values are assigned to the fields as follows. For a textbox, since its domain is not known, all the data instances from the GS are attempted. For a selected field, its set of values is limited to those values which are "similar" to the data instances in the GS. A value of a selected field is "similar" to a data instance if they have a common term. For a query interface, the maximum number of query submissions is the product of the number of attributes in the GS, the number of sample instances, and the number of fields in the interface. The result pages of all query submissions are stored and analyzed. This approach requires a data extraction system [Chang et al., 2006] and it uses the one described by Wang and Lochovsky [2003] to extract the data into a table whose columns correspond to the attributes of the RS.

Occurrence Matrix

Next we need to analyze the collection of result pages and count the occurrences of the query values in the result pages. We construct a 3-dimensional *occurrence matrix* (*OM*), where the first dimension is the set of the attributes in GS, the second dimension is the set of the attributes in IS, and the third one is the set of the attributes in RS. A cell $OM[i, j, k]$ contains the total occurrence count of observed query values in the kth attribute of RS when all the sample query values from the ith

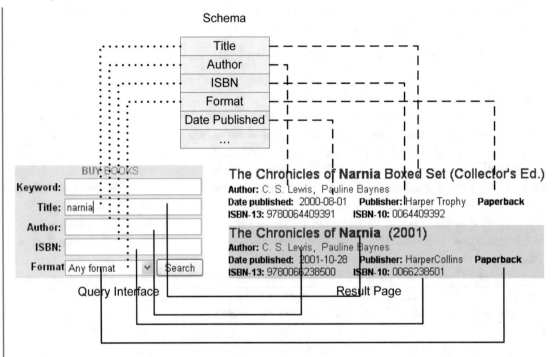

Figure 4.6: An example of a deep website with its query interface and result page.

attribute of GS are submitted to the jth attribute of IS. The 3-dimensional *OM* provides a unified solution to match the three pairs of Web database schemas. Next we present how *OM* is used to infer the matches. First, we describe how to match the attributes of IS and those of RS, those of IS and those of GS and the attributes of RS and those of GS. Then, we discuss how to obtain the matches between the ISs and between the RSs of two deep Web sites.

Table 4.2: An Example of *OM* Matrix with All Matches Highlighted

	Title$_{GS}$	Author$_{GS}$	Publisher$_{GS}$	ISBN$_{GS}$
Author$_{IS}$	93	498	534	0
Title$_{GS}$	451	345	501	0
Publisher$_{IS}$	62	184	468	275
Keyword$_{IS}$	120	248	143	275
ISBN$_{IS}$	0	0	0	258

Intra-Site Schema Matching

Let N be the number of attributes in GS, M be the number of elements in IS, and L be the number of columns in the result table. Using the *sum* projection function, we project OM into 2-dimensional occurrence matrices: $OM_{M \times N}^{IG}$ for IS and GS, $OM_{M \times L}^{IR}$ for IS and RS, and $OM_{N \times L}^{GR}$ for GS and RS. Table 4.2 shows an example $OM_{5 \times 4}^{IG}$ matrix with the correct matches highlighted. The analysis of this matrix highlights some properties of the matrix in connection with the matching problem. We first note that the highest occurrence count may not necessarily correspond to a correct match. For instance, the cell for Author$_{IS}$ and Publisher$_{GS}$ has the largest value in the matrix, but the two attributes do not semantically correspond to each other. Second, the relative magnitude of the value of a cell among the cells in its row and column is more indicative of a possible match than its absolute value. For instance, the value of the cell Publisher$_{IS}$ and Publisher$_{GS}$ is not the largest in the column of Publisher$_{GS}$, but it is relatively larger than any of the values in the row of Publisher$_{IS}$. The algorithm uses the *mutual information* to determine the correct matches. The mutual information measures the mutual dependence between two random variables X and Y, which is defined as:

$$MI(X, Y) = \Pr(X, Y) \log_2 \frac{\Pr(X, Y)}{\Pr(X) \Pr(Y)} . \tag{4.8}$$

In this approach, X is an attribute in IS, while Y is an attribute in GS. The probabilities $\Pr(X, Y)$, $\Pr(X)$ and $\Pr(Y)$ are computed using the values in the matrix. Suppose that X and Y correspond to the ith row and j^{th} column in $OM_{M \times N}^{IG}$. Let $M = \sum_{i,j} m_{ij}$, where m_{ij} is the entry in row i and column j in $OM_{M \times N}^{IG}$. Let $m_{i+} = \sum_{j} m_{ij}$ and $m_{+j} = \sum_{i} m_{ij}$. Then $\Pr(X, Y) = \frac{m_{ij}}{M}$, $\Pr(X) = \frac{m_{i+}}{M}$ and $\Pr(Y) = \frac{m_{+j}}{M}$. For example, $\Pr(\text{Publisher}_{IS}, \text{Publisher}_{GS}) = 0.025$ in Table 4.2. Using $OM_{M \times N}^{IG}$ we can compute the corresponding $MI_{M \times N}^{IG}$. The ith attribute of IS and the jth attribute of GS match if the entry e_{ij} of $MI_{M \times N}^{IG}$ is the largest among all the values in the ith row and the jth column.

Inter-Site Schema Matching

We now discuss how to find the corresponding attributes for the ISs and RSs of different Web databases. We discuss the matching of two ISs. RSs are matched in similar fashion. Let I_1 and I_2 be the interface schemas of two Web databases. Let $OM_{M \times N}^{I_1 G}$ and $OM_{M \times N}^{I_2 G}$ be the query occurrence matrices of the two Web databases, respectively. A *vector space model* [Salton and McGill, 1983] is used to match the attributes of two ISs. If each attribute in an IS is viewed as a "document" and each attribute of the GS is viewed as a "concept," then each row in either $OM_{M \times N}^{I_1 G}$ or $OM_{M \times N}^{I_2 G}$ represents a corresponding document vector. The similarity between an attribute in I_1 and another from I_2 is computed by the *Cosine* measure between their corresponding vectors (rows). We construct a matrix VS such that $VS(i, j)$ is the value of the *Cosine* measure between the ith attribute of I_1 and j^{th} attribute of I_2. A matrix entry in VS whose value is the largest both in its row and its column represents a match.

4.5.2 GATHERING INSTANCES FROM THE WEB

The above matching schemes work reasonably well and their accuracy can reach as high as 90%. One way to improve the accuracy of matching is to obtain instances of attributes that do not have instances in the query interfaces (i.e., textboxes). Specifically, for those attributes, we seek to find instances from the Web and utilize them for matching. Two solutions for gathering data instances for textboxes are described in Section 3.1.3. In particular, the solution proposed in WebIQ [Wu et al., 2006a] (Section 3.1.3) is motivated by query interface matching. The results show that acquired instances improve matching accuracy from 89.5% (F1-measure) [Wu et al., 2004] to 97.5% over the same data set of query interfaces.

CHAPTER 5

Query Interface Attribute Integration

After attribute matching discussed in the previous chapter, attributes in different query interfaces that are semantically equivalent have been identified. In this chapter, we discuss issues related to the integration of the matching local attributes into a single attribute in the integrated query interface. We call the attributes in the integrated query interface *global attributes*.

Each attribute in a Web-based query interface has a number of features, including its label (i.e., name), its domain type (e.g., whether it can take values from an infinite set or a finite set), values (for non-text input attribute), format (textbox, selection list, checkboxes, radio buttons), etc. Therefore, when we integrate the matching attributes, we also need to integrate all their features. These attribute integration issues are covered in this chapter.

In this chapter, we first review the attribute integration problem in traditional database context. The Web query interface integration problem is similar to the database schema integration problem. Therefore, naturally, the problem of attribute integration across multiple database schemas has been discussed before. Different attribute integration issues in traditional database schema context will be reviewed in Section 5.1. The rest of the chapter covers issues that are more specific to attribute integration in the context of the query interface integration of Web databases. In Section 5.2, we discuss two issues related to schema-level attribute integration. The first is how to automatically determine the label of the global attribute for a set of matching attributes in local query interfaces. The second is how to determine the domain type for each global attribute. In Section 5.3, we discuss how to integrate the values of the matching local attributes. We consider two types of values separately, one is of numerical type and the other is of non-numerical type.

5.1 TRADITIONAL ATTRIBUTE INTEGRATION

Attribute integration in the context of traditional database schema integration received considerable attention in the 1990s. A significant research issue in building multidatabase systems and/or heterogeneous database systems is *schema integration*, which aims to create a global schema on top of the schemas of the component databases of a multidatabase or heterogeneous database system. Once corresponding attributes in different local schemas have been matched, they need to be integrated into a global attribute in the global schema. Issues in the traditional attribute integration are centered on resolving various possible conflicts that may exist among the matching attributes.

The features of a typical attribute *A* of a database schema (say, relational database) include the name, data type, value precision, value unit, default value (optional), whether its values are unique (i.e., whether it is a key), whether null values are allowed, and check constraint(s) on values. Matching attributes from different local schemas may have conflict on each of these features, and when conflicts occur, they need to be resolved during attribute integration [Kim et al., 1995; Ram and Ramesh, 1999]. The integration of the values of the matching local attributes is also considered sometimes in attribute integration [Yu and Meng, 1997]. The resolution of conflict on each of the above features is discussed below.

1. *Name.* If all of the matching local attributes have the same name, just use this name as the name of the global attribute. If different names are used by these local attributes, a name can be suggested for the global attribute and the correspondence between the global name and each local name can be added to a mapping table.

2. *Data type.* If all of the matching local attributes have the same data type, just use this data type for the global attribute. If different data types are used by these local attributes, a technique known as *type coercion* [Kim et al., 1995] can be applied to resolve the conflict. This technique consists of a set of type coercion rules for coercing the data type of one attribute to another data type (i.e., the data type of the global attribute). This essentially causes the conversion of retrieved local attribute values to those of the global data type. For example, if the data type of a local attribute is char(9) and its values are all numbers and the data type selected for the global attribute is integer, then the retrieved values of digit strings from the local attribute will be converted to integers when they are presented to the users or applications of the multidatabase system.

3. *Value precision.* Conflict in value precision occurs when matching local attributes draw values from domains with different cardinalities [Kim et al., 1995]. For example, of the two matching local attributes for student grade, one has letter grade values A, B, C, D, and F, and another has number grade values between 0 and 100. This type of conflict can be resolved by defining a mapping between the values of the two attributes. For example, number grade values between 90 and 100 are mapped to A, those between 75 and 89 to B, and so on. With the defined mapping, the values of any of the matching local attributes can be used as the values of the global attribute.

4. *Different expressions of the same information.* This refers to the case where different scalar values are used to represent the same data. One such example is when different code values are used to denote the same meaning. For instance, the performance of employees in one database is denoted by values *excellent, good, fair, poor,* and *fail,* but in another database, it is denoted by 1, 2, 3, 4, and 5, respectively. This type of conflict can be resolved in a similar manner as that for *value precision,* i.e., by defining a mapping between the values.

5. *Value unit.* The values under different matching local attributes may be in different units, which cause a conflict on value unit. For example, product weight in one component database is in pound and in another is in kilogram. This type of conflict can usually be resolved by defining an arithmetic expression or a mapping table to convert numeric values in one unit to those of another. With the conversion expression or the mapping table defined, any of the units of the matching local attributes can be used for the global attribute. Note that some semantically related units do not have fixed conversion relationship. One such example is different currency units (e.g., U.S. dollar vs. Canadian dollar). In this case, a dynamic mapping table needs to be maintained.

6. *Default value.* In database systems, a default value for a certain attribute may be defined when tuples are added to a table. For multidatabase systems that do not support adding tuples, there is no need to have this feature. If insertion is supported, a default value could be used. If the default values defined for different matching local attributes are the same or can be mapped to the same global value after some of the aforementioned conflicts have been resolved, then this value can be used for the global attribute. If different default values are defined for different matching local attributes and these values cannot be mapped to the same value, then no default value should be defined for the global attribute.

7. *Uniqueness.* In general, even if the values under each of the matching local attributes are guaranteed to be unique, the same value may still appear in multiple of these local attributes. But if these matching attributes are used to join (including outerjoin) the tuples from the local tables to generate the set of tuples for the corresponding global table, then this attribute can still be defined as the key of the global table.

8. *Nullness.* If all matching local attributes allow null value, null value is also allowed for the global attribute. Otherwise, it is not allowed.

9. *Check constraint.* After the other conflicts have been resolved, the union of the check constraints defined on the matching local attributes is used for the global attribute, which allows the global check constraint to accommodate values from all matching local attributes. For example, consider two matching attributes A1 and A2. Suppose A1 has check constraint (A1 > 100) and A2 has check constraint (A2 < 50). Then the check constraint of the global attribute A should be (A > 100 or A < 50).

Note that some of the above features are insignificant for the global attribute if the said multidatabase system does not support update (including insert and delete) operations. These features include default value and check constraint, and to some extent uniqueness and nullness (the latter two may be useful when the retrieved data are to be fed into an application).

Sometimes the matching local attributes may have different values for the same entity. This is called *data inconsistency* [Meng and Yu, 1995]. Apparent data inconsistency does not necessarily mean one of the involved values must be incorrect. For example, that the same person having two different values under the matching salary attributes may be caused by the fact that this person earned the two salaries from two different jobs. One way to resolve data inconsistencies is to apply a *resolution function* to the involved values for each entity [Yu and Meng, 1997]. For the above example about the salaries from different jobs, the appropriate resolution function would be the sum function, meaning that the global salary value for each person is the sum of the salary values from different jobs (i.e., the salary from each component database represents the salary for one job). Other resolution functions include *max*, *min*, *avg*, etc.

The number of matching local attributes considered in traditional attribute integration is small (usually two [Kim et al., 1995], because the number of databases to be integrated is small) and the conflicts are resolved manually.

Compared to traditional attribute integration, there are several new issues in attribute integration in the context of Web query interface integration because of the following reasons. First, attributes in query interfaces have some new features that do not occur for attributes in traditional databases. For example, attributes in query interfaces are implemented by HTML input control elements (textbox, selection list, radio buttons, and checkboxes) and they may have values in the query interface (i.e., values in selection lists or labels associated to a group of radio buttons or checkboxes). These values are different from the values in the backend database systems. They are usually categorical in nature, for example, ranges for numerical values instead of individual numbers. Second, the number of matching attributes involved in an integration task is often large (from tens to hundreds) compared to the situation in tradition attribute integration. This makes attribute integration for query interfaces more challenging and also makes it necessary to have highly automated solutions. Attribute integration in the context of query interfaces will be discussed in the next two sections.

5.2   GENERATING GLOBAL ATTRIBUTES

Let $LMA = \{LA_1, LA_2, ..., LA_n\}$ be the set of matching attributes having the same meaning across different query interfaces of a Web database integration system, where each LA_i is from a different query interface. Based on the discussion in Section 2.1.1 in Chapter 2, each attribute LA_i has a number of features, including its *label (or name)*, *layout position*, *domain type*, *default value*, *value type*, and *unit*. LA_i may also consist of one or more fields. Each field in turn has its own *label* (possibly empty), *format* (i.e., input type – textbox, select, radio, and checkbox), *internal name* (for query submission), set of *internal values* (for query submission and correspond to external values), *domain type*, *field type* (i.e., domain field or constraint field), set of *external values*, and *default value* (may be null). When attribute LA_i has more than one field, the relationship among these fields can be one of the four types: *range type* (two input fields are used to specify a range of value), *part type* (for capturing the part-of relationship), *group type* (multiple checkboxes/radio buttons together form an attribute and labels of the check boxes/radio buttons become attribute values), and *constraint type* (some fields are used to specify constraints for another field).

When performing attribute integration, each feature of the matching attributes needs to be integrated. For example, the labels of the matching local attributes need to be integrated into a single attribute label for the global attribute. Among the features of an attribute, the *layout position* is a relative feature, i.e., the layout position of an attribute is relative to the layout positions of other attributes on the query interface. Therefore, it is more meaningful to consider the integration of layout positions for all attributes on query interfaces at the same time. We will delay the discussion on layout position integration to Chapter 6. In the following two subsections, we discuss how to integrate the labels and the domain types of the matching attributes. In Section 5.3, we discuss how to integrate the external values of the matching attributes. Note that we do not cover the integration of some of the attribute features because the integration of these features has not been reported in the literature. For example, some attributes have constraint fields that can be used to specify constraint on the search values specified in a domain field. As a concrete example, the attribute *Title Keywords* in Figure 2.2 (Chapter 2) has the constraint field "Exact Phrase," whereas the attribute *Title* in Figure 2.6 (Chapter 2) has the constraint fields "Title word(s)," "Start(s) of title word(s)," and "Exact start of title." The two attributes are clearly semantically equivalent in the book domain and, thus, their constraints should be integrated as well. We are not aware of any published work regarding the integration of such constraints.

5.2.1 GLOBAL ATTRIBUTE LABEL SELECTION

Let $LS = \{L_1, L_2, ..., L_n\}$ be the bag of labels of the matching attributes from different local query interfaces and let L be the label of the corresponding global attribute. The objective here is to determine L among LS. A simple solution is to select the label in LS that appears the most times. This is reasonable as the label with the highest frequency represents the most popular choice by the developers of the local query interfaces.

If two or more labels have the same highest frequencies, the one that is more general can be selected. The determination of which label is more general can be carried out as follows. First, hyponym hierarchies among the distinct labels in LS are first created. If label L_i is a hyponym of label L_j, make L_i a child of L_j in a hierarchy. WordNet [Fellbaum, 1998] can be used to identify the hyponym relationship between terms. If a label has no hypernym relationships with other labels, the label itself is considered as a hierarchy with a single (root) node. In general, multiple hierarchies may be formed from the distinct labels in LS. Next, the hierarchy with the highest frequency is selected and the label at the root of this hierarchy is chosen as L. The frequency of a hierarchy is defined to be the sum of the frequencies of the labels in the hierarchy. If multiple hierarchies have the same frequencies, then one of them can be selected arbitrarily. The basic idea of the above method was first proposed by He et al. [2003].

When the query interfaces are represented as hierarchical schemas (see Chapter 2), another consideration for selecting the label for each global attribute is that the label should be consistent with labels of its neighboring attributes as well as its descendant and ancestor attributes. This issue will be discussed in detail in Chapter 6.

After the global attribute label for each set of matching local attribute labels is selected, an attribute-mapping table is constructed, which records mappings from every local attribute label to its corresponding global attribute label. This mapping table will be used when translating global queries to local queries.

5.2.2   INTEGRATION OF DOMAIN TYPE

As described in Chapter 2, the query interface representation model proposed by He et al. [2003] has four attribute domain types and they are *range, finite, infinite,* and *Boolean.* The range type may be implemented by one or two fields (see Figure 5.3). The finite type may be implemented in three possible ways, i.e., a selection list, a group of checkboxes, and a group of radio buttons. The infinite type is implemented as a textbox. The Boolean type is a single checkbox or a single radio button. When integrating an attribute, a method is needed to determine a domain type that is compatible with the domain types of all the matching local attributes for the global attribute. The domain type determines the way the fields of the global attribute are presented in the integrated query interface, and how query conditions could be specified on the global attribute.

It is possible for matching attributes to have different domain types. For example, the *subject* attributes (including some matching attributes, same below) in some query interfaces of book Web databases have finite domains (i.e., they have pre-compiled values) while some other *subject* attributes have infinite domains (i.e., they allow users to enter a subject value). Even when matching attributes have the same domain type, they may still be implemented differently. For example, for two matching attributes of finite type in two query interfaces, one may be implemented as a selection list and another as a group of radio buttons. Therefore, domain type integration should address two issues, i.e., how to determine the domain type of the global attribute for each set of matching local attributes and how to determine its implementation. The two issues are addressed below.

There are two desirable requirements for determining the domain type of the global attribute. First, the chosen domain type should be compatible with all the domain types of the matching local attributes. Second, the chosen domain type should allow the information (e.g., the external values) available from the matching local attributes to be maximally utilized. Unfortunately, these two requirements cannot always be satisfied if only one of the above four domain types (i.e., *range, finite, infinite,* and *Boolean*) can be used for the global attribute. The example below illustrates this problem.

Example 5.1   Consider two matching local attributes A and B such that A has a finite domain type and B has an infinite domain type. For this example, none of the four domain types is a good choice for the integrated global attribute. Range and Boolean are obviously not suitable. Finite would not be compatible with the infinite domain type of B as the finite domain type does not permit a user to enter an un-prespecified value for the integrated global attribute, which may match some records in the Web database having B. Infinite domain type for the global attribute is compatible with the domain types of both A and B, but it does not utilize the prespecified external values under A, which makes it not satisfying the second requirement.

One method to resolve the above problem is to introduce a *hybrid domain type* for global attributes [He et al., 2003]. This hybrid domain type is a combination of the finite domain type and the infinite domain type. Specifically, it consists of two input control elements, one is a selection list corresponding to the finite domain type and the other is a textbox corresponding to the infinite domain type (see Figure 5.1). With the hybrid domain type, a user can either select a value from a list of prespecified values, which fully utilize the external values from local attribute A in the above example, or fill in a new value into the textbox if the value is not in the selection list. A user can only enter search values into one of the two input control elements at a time.

Figure 5.1: Hybrid domain type.

Given a number of matching local attributes, the following four rules can be used to determine the domain type of the global attribute [He et al., 2003]:

1. If all the matching attributes have the same domain type, then the global attribute also has this domain type.

2. If one of the matching attributes has a range type, then the domain type of the global attribute is also range. In this case, any non-range domain type of a matching attribute, if exists, can be viewed as a special range type with each value being treated as a single value range (e.g., 5 becomes [5, 5]). If all the matching attributes are finite, the range type of the global attribute is also finite. If one or more of the attributes are the infinite type (one or two textboxes are used for entering search ranges), then a hybrid range type (similar to the hybrid domain type described above) becomes the domain type of the global attribute.

3. If the matching attributes have mixed finite, infinite, Boolean, and hybrid domain types with at least one of them being either infinite or hybrid, then the domain type of the global attribute is hybrid.

4. If the matching attributes have mixed finite and Boolean domain types, then the domain type of the global attribute is finite.

After the domain type of a global attribute is determined, it is easy to find a valid implementation for it. For example, one strategy is as follows: (1) implement a finite type as a selection list; (2) implement an infinite type as a textbox; (3) implement a finite range type as a selection list of ranges and a hybrid range type using a mix of a selection list and textbox(es); (4) implement a hybrid domain type as shown in Figure 5.1; and (5) implement a Boolean type as a checkbox.

5.3 DOMAIN VALUE INTEGRATION

If multiple matching local attributes have values in their query interfaces, these values need to be merged to form the values for the integrated global attribute. The basic requirements for value integration are threefold. First, the merged values should be semantically unique. This requirement has two implications: (1) each value can only appear once in the global attribute even if it appears in multiple matching local attributes; and (2) no two values in the global attribute are semantically equivalent. Second, each value in the global attribute should match at least one local value. Third, every local value should correspond to at least one global value. The last two requirements are to ensure that every global value comes from some local value and every local value is represented by at least one global value.

Numerical and non-numerical values have different properties. For example, numerical values can form ranges while non-numerical values usually do not. Dates will be treated as numerical values in this chapter. Therefore, it is more appropriate to deal with the integration of these two types of values separately.

5.3.1 INTEGRATION OF NON-NUMERICAL DOMAINS

If some of the matching local attributes are of the *finite* domain type and have alphabetic values, these values need to be merged to form a value set for the global attribute. In the method used in WISE-Integrator [He et al., 2004c], the merging is carried out in two phases. In the first phase, a number of matching techniques (i.e., exact match, approximate string match, synonymy match, and hypernymy match) are employed to identify semantic relationships between values that appear in the matched local attributes. In the second phase, the relationships between the values are used to merge them and generate a value set for the global attribute.

The second phase consists of the following three steps.

1. Perform clustering on the values of matching local attributes. Synonymy match, approximate string match, and Cosine similarity match can be used to perform the clustering.

2. Choose one value in each cluster to represent the values in the cluster. The values in each cluster are considered to have similar meanings and the chosen value is a candidate global value to represent values in this cluster. A simple way is to choose the most popular value (i.e., the one that appears in most matching local attributes) in each cluster.

3. Perform hypernymy match among the candidate global values and determine the final global values for the corresponding global attribute. Two cases can be considered. First, there are no hypernymy relationships among the candidate global values. In this case, the candidate global values become the final global values. Second, there are hypernymy relationships among the candidate global values. Values not involved in any hypernymy relationships will become final global values. Now the question is how to properly handle each hypernymy hierarchy that is formed. Let H be such a hierarchy. There are three possible ways to choose final global

value(s) from H and different choices will have different effects on *query cost* and *interface friendliness*. The cost of evaluating a global query (i.e., a query against the integrated query interface) includes the cost of invoking local Web databases to accept sub-queries mapped from the global query, the cost of processing sub-queries at local Web databases, the cost of transmitting the results from local Web databases to the integration system and the cost of further processing the local results (e.g., result extraction and merging). The three possible choices are described below.

(a) Choose the most general concept (i.e., the value at the root of H) as the final global value to represent the values in H. With this choice, a global query may need to be mapped to multiple values (corresponding to the more specific values in H) in some local query interfaces, leading to multiple invocations to the local Web databases, and thereby higher query evaluation cost.

(b) Choose the most specific values (i.e., values at the leaf nodes) in H as the final global values to represent the values in H. In this case, users who want to query more general values (i.e., have broader coverage) may have to submit multiple queries using the more specific values, resulting in a less user-friendly interface.

(c) Keep all values in H, i.e., provide a *hierarchy* of values as the final global values. This choice remedies the problems of the previous two options and gives the users more flexibility to form their queries. More specifically, if a user wants to perform a narrow search for this attribute, the user can select a more specific value in H, which avoids mapping the value to unnecessary local values. On the other hand, if the user wants to perform a broader search, he/she can select a more general value in H, which relieves the user from the need of selecting multiple values or submitting multiple queries.

No matter which of the above options is chosen, the choice should be the same for all hypernymy hierarchies of the values of a global attribute. For example, if the most general value is chosen for one hierarchy, then the same option (first one above) should be chosen for all hierarchies.

Example 5.2   Consider two matching local attributes from the query interfaces of two Web book sites. One attribute, *Subjects*, has values "Network," "Databases," "Programming languages," and so on, and the other attribute, *Subject*, has values "TCP/IP," "Wireless network," "Oracle," "Sybase," "Sql server," "C," "C++," "Java," "Pascal," and so on. The two attributes and their values are shown in Figure 5.2. There are several hypernymy relationships among the values from the two attributes, including: "Network" is a hypernym of "TCP/IP" and "Wireless network," "Databases" is a hypernym of "Oracle," "Sybase," and "Sql server," "Programming languages" is a hypernym of "C," "C++," "Java," and "Pascal," etc. There are three possible ways to generate the global values. One is to use only the more general values, i.e., values from the first query interface, namely "Network," "Databases," "Programming languages," etc. In this case, suppose a user wants to find information about Oracle. Since "Oracle" is not available, the user has to select "Databases" on the integrated query interface and submit the query. This global query will be mapped to three sub-queries for the second Web book site, namely "Oracle," "Sybase," and "Sql server." Obviously, searching based on "Sybase" and "Sql server" will waste the resources at this website and return useless results to the integration system. The second option is to use only the more specific values, i.e., the values from the second interface. In this case, a user who wants to find information about a database (not of any specific type) needs to submit three queries using, respectively, "Oracle," "Sybase," and "Sql server." This is inconvenient to the user. The third option simply uses the hypernymy hierarchies (see the box on the right in Figure 5.2). In this case, if the user selects "Databases," the integration system will generate three sub-queries for the second site on behalf of the user. On the other hand, if any of the three hyponym values of "Databases" is selected, only that value will be used for the second website but "Databases" will be used for the first website. This option remedies the problems of the first two options.

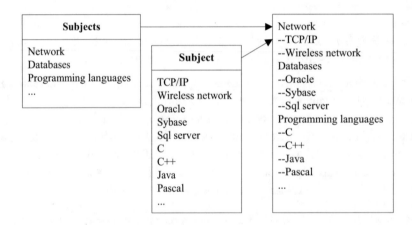

Figure 5.2: An example for integrating non-numerical domains.

5.3.2 INTEGRATION OF NUMERICAL DOMAINS

To integrate values of numeric domains, the following issues need to be tacked:

1. *Resolve unit difference.* Different units are sometimes used across different websites and these differences may also appear in query interfaces. Often they occur for measures such as length, weight, speed, and so on. For example, the weight of a product may be given in pounds in one query interface but in kilograms in another query interface. The differences need to be resolved before the involved values can be integrated.

2. *Understand the semantics of special terms, phrases, and symbols for specifying ranges.* Numerical range values often involve special terms, phrases, and, sometimes, special symbols. For example,

the meaning of "under" is "less than;" "from" and "to" are used to specify the lower and upper boundaries of a range, respectively; hyphen "-" is frequently used to specify a range. The meanings of these terms, phrases, and symbols need to be identified in advance.

3. *Generate the numerical values for the global attribute and determine the format for the global attribute.*

The first issue can be addressed by creating a mapping table in advance. Each entry in this table maps one unit of a measure to another unit of the measure. For example, for weight, one pound can be mapped to 0.453 kilograms. Some units, such as currency, may need dynamic mapping as the converting rates may change frequently. With this mapping table, values in different units across different matching local attributes can be converted to values of the same unit in the query interface representation schema of each local query interface. Numerical value integration will be performed based on the converted values. Note that when a global query is mapped to a local query for a local query interface, each global value in the global query needs to be converted back to local values of the right unit for the local query interface.

In general, two types of numeric domains can be differentiated: *range numeric domain* and *non-range numeric domain*. If the domains of the matching local attributes are all *non-range numeric*, the values of the global attribute can simply be the union of the numerical values of these matching attributes. For the rest of this subsection, we focus on attributes of *range numeric domain*. In the case where some matching local attributes have range values and some have non-range values, all non-range values are treated as special range values of the form $[v, v]$.

We now address how to deal with the special terms, phrases, and symbols for specifying ranges. These terms/phrases/symbols will be called *range specifiers* in this section. A variety of range specifiers can be seen in Figure 5.3. Ranges are often formed using numeric values and range specifiers together. To help the integration program understand different ranges, the meanings of different range specifiers need to be clearly defined to the program. This can be accomplished by building a semantic dictionary of commonly used range specifiers with clearly defined meanings. A portion of this dictionary is shown in Table 5.1.

In general, two pieces of information need to be considered when determining the specific range of a range value: the range specifier(s) used and the boundary value(s) used.

The last issue for integrating range values is to generate the global range values that are compatible with the local range values of the matching attributes and determine the format of the global attribute. In general, choosing a larger range for a global attribute on the integrated interface will likely lead to more queries for some local Web databases and thus a higher overall cost for evaluating the global query. Therefore, we should avoid having overly large ranges on the integrated interface. One approach [He et al., 2003] is to first obtain all the distinct (boundary) values from the matching local attributes, then sort these values in ascending order, and finally generate range values by treating these distinct values as boundaries, i.e., form a range value using every two consecutive

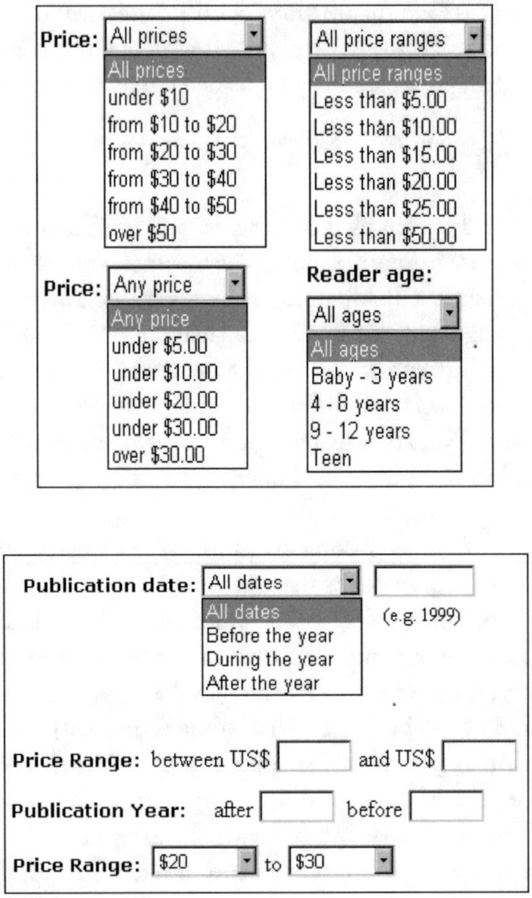

Figure 5.3: Examples of different range formats.

boundary values. In this approach, each range value between two boundary values v_1 and v_2 is represented by "from v_1 and v_2"; the range below the smallest boundary value and that above the largest boundary value are implemented using "under" and "over" range specifiers, respectively. If all range values of a global attribute can be determined, a single selection list can be used to implement the global range domain.

Example 5.3 Suppose in Figure 5.3 the two attributes with "from ...to ..." and "less than" range specifiers are matched. The list of distinct numeric values under the two attributes is: 5, 10, 15, 20, 25, 30, 40, 50. Using these values as boundaries, the range values for the global attribute can be easily obtained (see the values in the rightmost box in Figure 5.4).

Table 5.1: Range Specifiers and Their Meanings

Range Specifiers	Meaning	
less than	$<$	
greater than	$>$	
over	$>$	
under	$<$	
below	$<$	
above	$>$	
from	$\geq$	⎫ Used in pair
to	$\leq$	⎭
before	$<$	
after	$>$	
between	$\geq$	⎫ Used in pair
and	$\leq$	⎭
$(v_1) - (v_2)$	$(v_1) \leq \ldots \leq (v_2)$	
...	...	
all	full range	
any	full range	

The above simple approach for generating global range values has a nice feature, that is, each global range value is mapped to at most one local range value on each local query interface. This means that a query condition on such a global attribute will not lead to multiple local queries on any local query interface. On the other hand, there are two problems with this approach. The first is that it tends to produce a large number of small range values for the global attribute, especially when the number of matching local attributes is large. This causes some inconvenience for users who want to specify a large range in their global queries. The second problem is that the global range values so produced are likely to be proper sub-ranges of local range values. This leads to over-retrieval by local Web databases, meaning that a significant amount of postprocessing is needed at the integration system to filter out invalid results returned by local Web databases.

The first problem can be alleviated by introducing another level of range values on top of current range values to create range hierarchies. For example, each higher-level range value can be

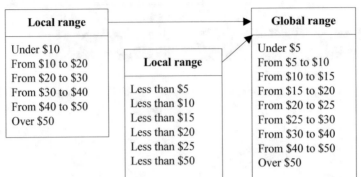

Figure 5.4: An example of integrating range-numerical domains.

formed by grouping k current range values at the lower level for some integer k. The higher-level and lower-level range values correspond to more general terms and more specific terms for non-numerical values in Section 5.3.1 and their usages are also similar. Global queries that need wider ranges can select higher-level range values while those that need narrower ranges can select lower-level range values. The second problem can be addressed partially by analyzing the *interface frequency* of each local range value, which is the number of query interfaces that contain the local range value. High-frequency local range values should be preserved in the global attribute as much as possible, which increases the chance a global range value will match a single local range value exactly, reducing the need to perform postprocessing filtering.

Some details to the sketched solutions of the above two problems still need to be worked out. For example, how to group lower-level range values to higher-level ones in order to maximize the benefit and how to select local range values to preserve under the global attribute when multi-level range values are used? To the best of the authors' knowledge, these issues remain to be investigated.

The range value integration method proposed by He et al. [2003] only considered the situations where the range values for each matching local attributes are already provided in the local query interface. There are cases where this is not true, i.e., some or all of the matching local attributes do not have fully prespecified range values. This happens when one or two textboxes are used to implement the format of a range attribute. Several examples of such cases can be seen in Figure 5.3. If two textboxes are used for all matching local attributes, the global attribute should also be implemented using two textboxes. If some matching local attributes provide specific range values and some others have only two textboxes, then a sensible solution is to create a selection list of range values based on the prespecified local range values for the global attribute while at the same time also provide two textboxes for the global attribute (similar to the hybrid domain type introduced in Section 5.2.2). There does not seem to have a good solution for handling range attribute implementations that use one textbox and one set of prespecified values other than just including it (or them) as is in the global query interface. Fortunately, such implementations of range attributes are relatively rare.

CHAPTER 6

Query Interface Integration

Once we have computed the matching between the attributes of a set of query interfaces in the same application domain (e.g., book, airline, real estate), we can attempt to automatically construct a *global query interface* (GQI) for the domain. The GQI permits users to uniformly access information from local Web databases in the domain. The global interface must resemble the "look and feel" of the local interfaces as much as possible despite being automatically generated (i.e., without human support). In this chapter, we describe the process of constructing a GQI from the query interfaces of local Web databases of the same domain. Several query interface integration algorithms have been proposed [Dragut et al., 2006a,b; He and Chang, 2006; He et al., 2004a,c; Wu et al., 2004]. Early works [He and Chang, 2006; He et al., 2004a; Wu et al., 2004] on the problem have only aimed to find a unified model, which gives the structure of the attributes across all sources (e.g., "From City," "Departure Location," and "From Airport" are the same concept in the Airfare domain, and so are "Number of Connections" and "Stops"). Subsequent works have noticed that, for query interfaces to be user-friendly, they exhibit important structural relationships between their attributes. As a result, these relationships need to be reflected as much as possible on a GQI. For example, following the observation that each attribute has its layout position on its own source interface, WISE-Integrator [He et al., 2004c] estimates the layout of the attributes on a GQI by aggregating the positions of the attributes on the local interfaces. Therefore, the attributes of the GQI which appear in high positions (the first position is the highest) in many local interfaces will likely appear in high positions in the GQI, and the attributes that rarely appear in local interfaces will likely be positioned near the bottom of the GQI. WISE-Integrator also considers the problems of generating the domains of the attributes of a GQI (Chapter 5) and of finding suitable names for the attributes of a GQI. By considering query interfaces as schema trees, Dragut et al. [2006a,b] showed that the user-friendliness can be more systematically captured and reflected during the construction of a GQI. The content of this chapter is mainly drawn from their integration algorithm.

We first lay down a set of properties that facilitates a precise characterization of a GQI and that provides the bases for systematic construction of a GQI. Three major components contribute to a *well-designed* query interface [Dragut et al., 2006b]: *structural*, *lexical*, and *values*. The *structural component* was discussed at length in Chapter 2. To summarize, from a structural perspective the fields of a query interface are organized in *groups* (semantic units) [Dragut et al., 2006a; Zhang et al., 2004] so that semantically related fields are placed in the same group. For example, the fields *Adult, Senior, Child* in the interface in Figure 2.1 are placed together. In addition, related groups of fields are organized in super-groups (e.g., "When Do You Want to Go?"). This bottom-up grouping leads to a *hierarchical structure* for query interfaces, where a leaf node in the tree corresponds to an input

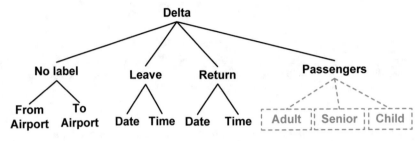

Figure 6.1: After field *passengers* is expanded into *adult*, *senior*, and *child*, it becomes an internal node.

field in the interface, an internal node corresponds to a (*super*) *group* of fields, and the order among the sibling nodes within the tree resembles the order of fields in the interface. In this chapter, we assume the hierarchical model for query interfaces (Chapter 2). That is, each interface is represented as a *schema tree*. The *lexical component* is concerned with the appropriateness of the text fields of an interface: The labels assigned to the fields of an interface need to be carefully chosen so as to convey both the meaning of each individual field and to underline the subordination organization of the fields (e.g., the fields *Adult*, *Senior*, and *Child* together with their parent "Number of Passengers" in Figure 2.1). The third component is *field values*. Designers rely on instances to further help users grasp the role of fields within a query interface. For example, the field *Adult* in Figure 2.1 has a set of predefined values. The quality of a GQI has to be judged along these three components. This chapter focuses on the structural and lexical components. The integration of values of matching fields was covered in Chapter 5.

The input to the query interface integration algorithm consists of:

A set of local query interfaces *LQI* in a given domain of interest,

A *mapping* that globally characterizes the semantic correspondences between equivalent fields across the query interfaces in *LQI*.

The mapping is organized in clusters (Section 3.1), that record 1:1 and 1:m matchings of fields. The GQI has one field per cluster.

The output of the integration algorithm is a query interface that consists of all (or the most significant) fields of all local interfaces and preserves as much as possible all the constraints enforced by the interfaces being merged. The constraints to be satisfied by the GQI are the structural and lexical constraints.

This chapter is organized as follows. Since query interface integration problem is an instance of the general problem of schema integration, we first give a brief overview of the traditional schema integration problem in Section 6.1. Then in Section 6.2, we describe the part of the query interface integration algorithm that addresses the structural component. In Section 6.3, we present the lexical component of the integration algorithm.

6.1   TRADITIONAL SCHEMA INTEGRATION

As mentioned in Section 4.1, in traditional schema integration, the schemas of multiple databases are integrated into a single global schema. Traditional database schema integration has been performed on input schemas in different data models [Ram and Ramesh, 1999] such as E-R model (e.g., Batini and Lenzerini, 1984), relational data model (e.g., Al-Faghi and Scheuermann, 1981), and object-oriented data model (e.g., Thieme and Siebes, 1993). In this section, we assume that all local schemas as well as the output schema (i.e., the global schema) are in the same data model – the relational data model. In other words, we focus on relational schema integration.

In traditional relational schema integration, each local database schema may consist of multiple inter-related relation schemas. At this time, we assume that semantically related relations from different local schemas have already been identified and all conflicts involving relation names, attribute names, and various attribute features have already been resolved (these issues are discussed in Chapters 4 and 5). Semantically related relations may be related in a number of ways: (1) they are semantically equivalent (e.g., all contain books of the same type), (2) one is more general than another (e.g., one contains books and another contains IT books), and (3) they share many properties and their names have a common, more general concept (e.g., one contains fictions and another contains IT books; the common more general concept is book).

Different integration operators can be used to integrate semantically related local relations from different local schemas. To simplify, in this section we restrict ourselves mostly to cases where two semantically related relations $R1$ and $R2$ are to be integrated. For a given relation S, we use $type(S)$, $extension(S)$, and $world(S)$ to represent the set of attributes, the set of tuples, and the set of real-world entities of S, respectively. All relations in the global schema, called *global relations*, are virtual relations as they do not have real data. But they do have tuples that conceptually belong to them.

We first consider the case where $R1$ and $R2$ are semantically equivalent and let R denote the global relation integrated from $R1$ and $R2$, i.e., $R = int\_op(R1, R2)$, where int_op represents the integration operator used. $R1$ and $R2$ have real tuples in them. After the integration, R will have a set of tuples that conceptually belong to R. We also use $extension(R)$ and $world(R)$ to denote the set of conceptual tuples and the set of conceptual entities of R, respectively. There are different ways to integrate $R1$ and $R2$ into R depending on more specific relationships between $R1$ and $R2$ [Yu and Meng, 1997] as shown below.

1. $type(R1) = type(R2)$. In this case, we define $R = \cup(R1, R2) = R1 \cup R2$. In other words, the union operator is used to integrate $R1$ and $R2$ into R. This results in $type(R) = type(R1)$, $extension(R) = extension(R1) \cup extension(R2)$ and $world(R) = world(R1) \cup world(R2)$.

2. $type(R1) \neq type(R2)$, $R1$ and $R2$ share the same key attribute(s) and $world(R1) \cap world(R2) = \emptyset$. In this case, we define $R = OU(R1, R2) = R1$ OU $R2$, where OU is the *outerunion* operation. Outerunion is similar to union except that the former does not require $type(R1) = type(R2)$. If a tuple t from $R1$ does not have an attribute A in $type(R2)$, a null value is

assigned to $t[A]$, which is the value of A in t, in the result of the outerunion. This results in $type(R) = type(R1) \cup type(R2), extension(R) = extension(R1) \cup extension(R2)$ and $world(R) = world(R1) \cup world(R2)$. It can be seen that union is a special case of outerunion.

3. $type(R1) \neq type(R2)$, $R1$ and $R2$ share the same key attribute(s) and $world(R1) \cap world(R2)$ $\neq \emptyset$. In this case, we define $R = OJ(R1, R2) = R1 \ OJ \ R2$, where OJ is the *outerjoin* operation. Outerjoin is similar to join except that it also keeps dangling (unmatched) tuples in each input relation in the result with padded null values for attributes these tuples do not have. With outerjoin, $type(R) = type(R1) \cup type(R2)$, $extension(R)$ consists of three sets of tuples, one is the set of tuples from joining $R1$ and $R2$ and the other two are dangling tuples (with padded null values) from $R1$ and $R2$ respectively, and $world(R) = world(R1) \cup world(R2)$.

We next consider the case where the concept for one relation (say $R1$) is more general than that of another (say $R2$). There are two ways to perform the integration. The first is to integrate $R2$ into $R1$. This is similar to the case where $R1$ and $R2$ are semantically equivalent in terms of its sub-cases except that the name of $R1$ is used as the name of R. One problem with this solution is that the ability to retrieve tuples from only $R2$ from the global schema is lost. For example, suppose $R1$ is *Books* and $R2$ is *IT_Books*. By integrating *IT_Books* into *Books*, we can no longer support retrieving only IT books from the global schema. One might think that we could retain the ability to retrieve only IT books by introducing an attribute such as *book_type* for the global *Books* (the values of the new attribute for books from *IT_Books* are IT). Unfortunately, this does not work when the global *Books* is only a schema without real tuples. The second solution which can avoid the problem of the above solution is to integrate $R2$ into $R1$ while at the same time keep $R2$ in the global schema. In other words, the global schema will have a global $R1$ and a global $R2$, where the global $R1$ is integrated from local $R1$ and local $R2$, while the global $R2$ is the same as the local $R2$ except that the global $R2$ only conceptually contains the tuples in the local $R2$. From the global $R1$, tuples from both local $R1$ and local $R2$ can be retrieved. From the global $R2$, tuples from local $R2$ can be retrieved. Note that having both $R1$ and $R2$ in the global schema does not lead to real redundancy, as the global $R1$ and $R2$ do not have real data.

The last case is when $R1$ and $R2$ have many common attributes and share a more general concept. Three sub-cases can be considered when integrating $R1$ and $R2$. One is not to integrate them and simply create their global version in the global schema, that is, the global $R1$ ($R2$) is mapped from the local $R1$ ($R2$). Another is to integrate them into a single global relation using one of the integration operators introduced earlier (i.e., union, outerunion, or outerjoin). This solution does not support retrieving from only one of the local relations from the global schema, which may be good for global users who are interested in tuples from $R1$ or $R2$ (e.g., fictions or IT books) only. A third solution is to create a new global relation $R = R1 \ Ge \ R2$, where Ge is called the *generalization operation* [Yu and Meng, 1997]. This operation is defined by $type(R) = type(R1) \cap type(R2)$, $extension(R) = \pi_{type(R)}(R1) \cup \pi_{type(R)}(R2)$, here π is the relational *project* operation, and $world(R) = world(R1) \cup world(R2)$. Since R does not contain all information from $R1$ and $R2$, the global versions of $R1$ and $R2$ are also created in the global schema.

When more than two relations from different local schemas are semantically related, their integrations can be performed in multiple steps in a certain order. For example, first integrate local relations that are semantically equivalent, then integrate local or integrated relations whose names have hypernymy or hyponymy relationships, and finally integrate local or integrated relations whose names share a more general concept.

In query interface integration, each local query interface conceptually consists of just one relation schema or one schema tree of fields. In this chapter, query interfaces are assumed to be represented as a hierarchy of fields. In this context, there are several new challenges for query interface integration that have not been discussed before in traditional database schema integration. For example, in traditional database schemas, the order of attributes in a relation is insignificant, but in the hierarchical representation of query interfaces, the order of the sibling fields under the same parent node is important and the order should be retained as much as possible during integration. As another example, the issue of having consistent attribute names within the same global relation has not been discussed in the context of database schema integration, but the consistency of names among siblings and across parent and child nodes in hierarchical query interface integration is important for better user experience with the integrated query interface. We also note that having redundant schema information in the global schema is often not a significant problem for database schema integration. For instance, when integrating two local relations with common attributes and a more general concept, the generalization operation can be used to generate a global relation schema that consists of the common attributes in the two local relations. In this case, the global versions of the two local relation schemas are also created in the global schema, causing the attributes common to both local relations to appear in multiple global relation schemas. This is a well accepted solution. But the integrated global query interface generally does not allow the same attributes (fields) to appear multiple times because otherwise the global query interface may become too complex to use for ordinary users. These and other challenges in query interface integration are addressed in the subsequent sections of this chapter.

6.2   QUERY INTERFACE MERGING

We describe an algorithm to compute the schema tree of a GQI from a set of query interfaces in the same domain. The algorithm has three steps. First, it structurally aligns the interfaces to be merged. Then, it computes the set of groups of semantically related fields of a GQI. It then merges the set of interfaces such that the groups of semantically related fields and the ancestor-descendant relationships among the fields within each interface are preserved as much as possible.

6.2.1   STRUCTURE ALIGNMENT

A granularity mismatch between two schemas occurs when there are 1:m mapping relationships between the fields of the schemas. In order to have a uniform representation of the fields within all the schemas, 1:m relationships are reduced to instances of 1:1 relationships. The resolution is done by expanding the leaf nodes on the one side of 1:m mapping into an internal node whose child nodes have 1:1 correspondence to the leaf nodes on the many side. Consider the example in Figure 6.1. The field *Passengers* in interface Delta participates in a 1:3 mapping relationship with the fields *Adult*, *Senior*, and *Child* of the interface in Figure 2.1 (Chapter 2). Thus, *Passengers* is expanded such that between the two interfaces there are only 1:1 correspondences. In the new organization of the interface Delta, *Passengers* is an internal node with three child nodes.

6.2.2   FIELD GROUPING

From a user's perspective the GQI is just another interface in the domain of discourse. Since the fields of the local query interfaces are organized into groups of semantically related fields (Chapter 2), the fields of the GQI should follow suit. The challenge of organizing the fields of a GQI into groups of semantically related fields lies in that the fields of the GQI originate from disparate interfaces, each interface potentially organizing its fields in a different way. It has been however observed that in each domain there are a few "inherent" ways of arranging the fields of a query interface [Dragut et al., 2006a; He and Chang, 2006]. This "hidden" property is used in the grouping algorithm that we will present in this section.

The *grouping constraint* is the requirement of constructing a GQI that accommodates all the sets of *adjacent sibling leaf nodes* of all query interfaces considered for integration. Intuitively, a *group* (of fields) within a GQI is a sequence of adjacent sibling leaf nodes derived from the sets of siblings of the local interfaces. For instance, in Figure 6.2, {leaveMonth, leaveDay} is a set of adjacent leaf nodes in the interface Delta, {depMonth, depDay, depTime} is a set of adjacent leaf nodes in AA and {dep_Month, dep_Day, dep_Year} is a set of adjacent leaf nodes in KLM. They lead to the group [depTime, depDay, depMonth, depYear] ([ ] denotes a *sequence*), where all the adjacent leaf nodes in the three sets remain adjacent. We use the internal names (i.e., the variable names that identify the fields in the HTML script) to qualify fields of the interface, because in this example the fields do not have labels. The grouping problem is the problem of partitioning the set of fields of the GQI into sets of semantically related fields. For instance, the groups for the example presented in Figure 6.2 are [From City, To City], [depTime, depDay, depMonth, depYear], [Senior, Adult, Child, Infant], [retYear, retTime, retDay, retMonth] and [Economy, Business Class & Higher] with each group denoting a set of fields that form a semantic unit of information.

In order to determine the organization of the fields within an integrated interface we introduce the notion of *adjacency constraint*. An *adjacency constraint* is a maximal set of adjacent sibling leaf nodes in a schema tree whose parent is not the root. For example, the interface AA in Figure 6.2 induces the following adjacency constraints: {From City, To City}, {depMonth, depDay, depTime}, {Adult, Senior, Child} and {Economy, Business Class}. A set of leaf nodes in a local schema tree whose parent is the root is not an adjacency constraint because an interface may have all its fields as child nodes of the root. Hence, no reliable information can be derived. The order of the fields within an adjacency constraint is ignored because it depends on various factors, such as the social and geographical contexts where the application is used (e.g., North America vs. Europe). For

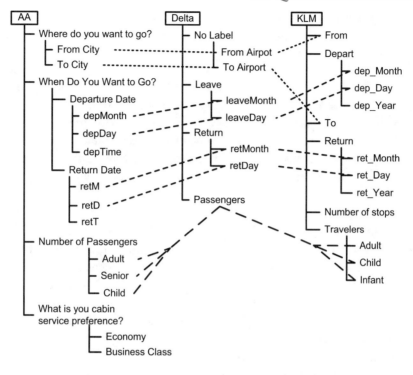

Figure 6.2: Three schema trees in the airfare domain along with the mapping between them.

example, the European format for date is day/month/year whereas the format used in the U.S. is month/day/year.

We now give a more precise definition of the notion of a group of fields in a GQI. Let Ω be the set of all the adjacency constraints induced by the interfaces in *LQI*. A subset of adjacency constraints $\Gamma \subseteq \Omega$ is a *group support* if (1) $\forall(\omega \in \Omega\backslash\Gamma, \omega' \in \Gamma)(\omega \cap \omega' = \emptyset)$ and (2) for any two adjacency constraints $\omega, \omega' \in \Gamma$, there exists a finite sequence of adjacency constraints $\omega_1, \ldots, \omega_n \in \Gamma$ such that $\omega_1 = \omega, \omega_n = \omega'$ and $\omega_i \cap \omega_{i+1} \neq \emptyset, 1 \leq i \leq n$. Let X be the union of the fields appearing in the adjacency constraints in Γ, i.e., $X = \bigcup_{\omega \in \Gamma} \omega$. A *group g* over the fields in X with the group support Γ is a permutation of X, X_{seq}, such that the fields of each adjacency constraint $\omega \in \Gamma$ are in adjacent positions in X_{seq}.

Example 6.1   Consider the example in Figure 6.2. $\Omega =$ {{From City, To City}, {From Airport, To Airport}, {From, Depart}, {leaveMonth, leaveDay}, {depMonth, depDay, depTime}, {dep_Month, dep_Day, dep_Year},…, {Adult, Child, Infant}}. An example of group support in Ω is $\Gamma =$ {{leaveMonth, leaveDay}, {depMonth, depDay, depTime}, {dep_Month, dep_Day, dep_Year}}. It is easy to check that Γ satisfies the above properties (1) and (2). X = {depMonth, depDay, depYear, dep-Time}. It is also easy to check that the permutation X_{seq} = [depTime, depDay, depMonth, depYear] satisfies the three adjacency constraints in Γ.

The algorithm to compute the set of groups for a GQI has the following steps. First, it collects all the adjacent constraints Ω from the local interfaces. Second, it partitions Ω into a set of group supports. Third, it determines whether each group support amounts to a group. If yes, the groups are reported. Otherwise, for each group support for which a group cannot be constructed, the algorithm finds a permutation that accommodates most of the adjacency constraints. The first two steps are relatively straightforward. The last step of the algorithm is described below.

Testing for Groups

Formally, the problem is as follows. Given a support group Γ and the set of all the fields X appearing in the adjacency constraints in Γ, find a permutation of X, X_{seq}, such that the fields of each adjacency constraint in Γ are in adjacent positions in X_{seq}. The problem is identical to the set-definition of the *Consecutive Ones Property* (C1P) [Booth and Lueker, 1976]. C1P is stated as follows. Given a universal set U and a subset B of the power set of U, we want a permutation π of the items of U such that all the items in each set in B appear as a consecutive sequence in π [Booth and Lueker, 1976]. In our problem, X corresponds to U, fields correspond to the items, Γ corresponds to the power set B, and the permutation X_{seq} corresponds to π.

The C1P exists if and only if a non-null *PQ-tree* can be constructed [Booth and Lueker, 1976]. PQ-Tree is a data structure for representing the permutations on a set U in which various subsets of U are constrained to occur consecutively. The fundamental elements of a PQ-Tree are P-Nodes and Q-Nodes. P-Nodes allow their child nodes to be permuted in any order, while Q-Nodes allow only a reversal of the ordering of their child nodes. These operations are referred to as *equivalence transformations*. Two PQ-Trees are deemed equivalent if one can be transformed into the other by applying zero or more equivalence transformations. The initial or universal PQ-Tree is created by adding all of the items of U as P-Node (leaf) child nodes of a root P-Node. The example depicted in Figure 6.3 shows (on the left) the universal tree for the set of fields {depDay, depMonth, depTime, depYear}. For the set of adjacent constraints {{leaveMonth, leaveDay}, {depMonth, depDay, depTime}, {depMonth, depDay, depYear}}, we obtain the PQ-tree shown in Figure 6.3 (on the right). A PQ-tree can be constructed in polynomial time. Other solutions have been proposed for solving C1P, most of them being variations or generalizations of PQ-tree, such as the PQR-tree [Meidanis et al., 1998].

A group can be constructed for a group support Γ and a set of fields X if and only if a PQ-tree exists. If the PQ-tree exists, a possible permutation is obtained by traversing the leaf nodes of the tree from left to right. For the example described in Figure 6.3, the permutation is [depTime, depDay, depMonth, depYear].

When a sequence X_{seq} with the above properties is not found, we look for a partial (optimal) solution. That is, we look for the permutation that satisfies the largest number of adjacency con-

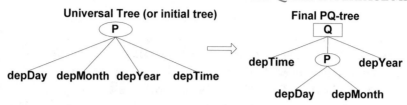

Figure 6.3: Illustrating the application of the PQ-tree.

straints. We however note that some adjacency constraints occur more often that the others. Hence, we need to collect the frequency of occurrence of each adjacency constraint among the schemas in *LQI*. As a result, each adjacency constraint $\omega \in \Omega$ also has a frequency of occurrence f_ω, which is the number of query interfaces in *LQI* having ω. When a permutation X_{seq} does not exist, we want to find a permutation X'_{seq} of X such that $f = \sum_{\omega \in \Gamma} f_\omega$ is maximized, where Γ is the set of adjacency constraints satisfied by X'_{seq}.

   This (more general) formulation of the problem is NP-hard [Dragut et al., 2006a]. The problem can be solved in a brute force manner in most practical cases, since X rarely exceeds seven fields and the computation is performed off-line.

   When a permutation X_{seq} does not exist meeting all the adjacency constraints in the associated group support, this is usually an indication that there is no apparent semantic relationship between all the fields in X. Thus, instead of computing X'_{seq}, we can alternatively try to determine the subsets of fields in X that are "likely" to be semantically related. This is accomplished by determining a way to split X in disjoint subsets of at least two fields such that the value of f is maintained. If such splits cannot be determined the original permutation is accepted as optimal. Notice that by splitting X in disjoint subsets we cannot obtain a larger value for f, and thus satisfying more adjacency constraints, because by concatenating back the splits we would obtain a permutation of X with a larger f value, which is a contradiction with f being the maximum.

Table 6.1: A Collection of Adjacency Constraints along with their Frequencies

Adjacency constraints	Frequency of occurrence
depDay, depMonth	7
depDay, depMonth, depTime	3
depMonth, depDay, depYear	4
depDay, Airline, Class	2

Consider an example consisting of the adjacency constraints as shown in the first column of Table 6.1. The second column of the table contains the frequency of occurrence of each adjacency constraint. Using the PQ-tree algorithm, it can be shown that no permutation satisfying all the adjacency constraints can be formed. By enumerating all permutations of the six fields {depTime, depDay, depMonth, depYear, Airline, Class}, the maximum number of constraints that can be satisfied is $f = 14$. And this is achieved by splitting the set into [depTime, depDay, depMonth, depYear] and [Airline, Class].

A GQI may have fields that do not belong to any group. Such fields are produced either by fields that appear as leaf child nodes of the root or as isolated child nodes of internal nodes, other than the root in all query interfaces in *LQI*. In the merging process, these two types of fields are treated differently. The former is discarded before the merge and the fields in this category are added as child nodes of the root of the integrated schema. For the latter we rely on the merge algorithm to find their appropriate locations within the integrated schema so as to preserve their ancestor-descendant relationships.

6.2.3   MERGING QUERY INTERFACES

Ancestor-descendant relationships among attributes in local query interfaces need to be preserved in the global query interface as they convey important semantic information. For instance, "Address" (along with its child nodes) in the query interface Chase (Figure 6.4) is a company address (rather than a home address) because "Address" is a descendant of "Employment Information." By preserving this hierarchical relationship within a GQI for the Credit Card domain, the user would also know that "Address" refers to the address of a company.

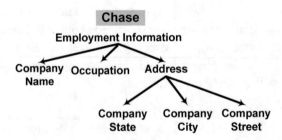

Figure 6.4: An example from the credit card domain.

In theory, there can be situations where some ancestor-descendant relationships cannot be preserved. For instance, in the Movie domain, the relationship between the Movies and Theaters entities can be represented as either Theaters running Movies, which makes Theaters an ancestor of Movies, or Movies played in Theaters, which makes Movies an ancestor of Theaters. Obviously, an integrated interface can only preserve one of the two relationships. Based on a study of about

700 query interfaces in 12 application domains, this was not found to be a problem [Dragut et al., 2009b], since not a single such case was observed.

The merging of a set of local schemas LQI is carried out pairwise. The schemas in LQI are first sorted in descending order of their heights and numbers of leaf nodes. The algorithm starts by merging the first two schemas in LQI. The resulted integrated schema is then merged with the third schema in LQI, and so on. The details of this algorithm are given below.

The Pairwise Merge Algorithm

We describe the process of merging two schemas $S, T \in LQI$, given the set of groups of fields G induced by the query interfaces in LQI. T is the *target schema* and S is the *source schema*. A heuristic is employed for this choice: between two schema trees the one with more levels is chosen as the target schema. If they have the same depth, the one with more leaf nodes is chosen. If a tie occurs, then one of them is randomly picked as the target schema.

The algorithm proceeds in a bottom-up fashion, starting from the level farthest from the root in S and progressing toward the root. For each node v at level l, if the node is a leaf, several sub-cases are considered. First, if v matches some field w in T, the algorithm simply combines v with w and moves to the next sibling of v. If v is an unmatched leaf node, then it checks the condition $\exists(g \in G)\exists(w \in T)(v, w \in g)$, i.e., whether there exists a leaf node w in T such that v and w are members of the same group g. Note that g is unique. If the condition is true, it inserts v into T next to w. Otherwise, the algorithm looks for the matching behavior among the siblings of v in order to find the proper insertion position for v in T. If its leftmost right (rightmost left) sibling v' matches a field u in T, v will be inserted into T as the left (right) sibling of u. It is possible that v and none of its siblings is matched. In this case, the algorithm postpones the insertion of v which will eventually be inserted into T with one of the subtrees containing it. It is also possible that v has a matching sibling other than the leftmost right (rightmost left) sibling. By the repeated application of the algorithm for the nodes in S at the same level with v, the leftmost right (rightmost left) sibling will eventually be matched to some node in T and thus v will be inserted into some location of T.

If v is an internal node at current level l, then either all of its child nodes have been matched or none of them has been matched, for if at least one child node of v has been matched, the remaining child nodes will be matched as described above. In such a situation, v will be combined with the lowest common ancestor of the matching nodes of its child nodes in T. This choice is critical to the preservation of ancestor-descendant relationship between the nodes of S in the integrated schema. If no child node of v is matched, then the whole subtree rooted at v will be inserted into T if a sibling of v has been matched.

The GQI of the three query interfaces in Figure 6.2 is shown in Figure 6.5. We start by merging AA and Delta. AA is the target. Their result is then merged with KLM. Having the groups, it is easy to find the positions of the fields Infant ret_Year and dep_Year from KLM in the GQI. The element "Number of stops" is inserted at the end of the merging process as a child node of the root of the integrated schema tree. Recall that leaf child nodes of the root are discarded before the merge.

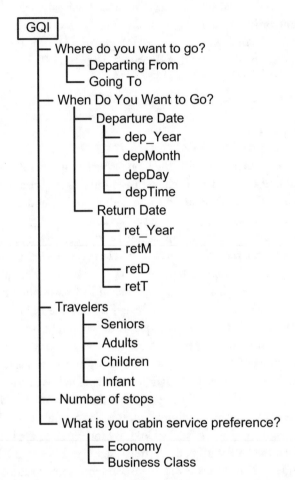

Figure 6.5: The merged query interface of the interfaces in Figure 6.2.

Post Processing

By repeatedly applying the above algorithm, the resulted integrated schema tree J complies with the ancestor-descendant relationships in each of the source schemas. It however may not satisfy all the groups. Two problems can occur in J: (1) the leaf nodes belonging to the same group do not share a common parent and (2) the leaf nodes in a group may share a parent, but they are not in the proper order. In the latter case the leaf nodes in each group are organized such that they obey the ordering suggested by the PQ-tree. The leftmost tree in Figure 6.6 illustrates (1): the leaf nodes a, b, c, and

d are in the same group, but they are not placed together. In case (1), for each group the leaf nodes of the group are placed in J such that they share the same parent, while simultaneously maintaining the ancestor-descendant relationships in the local interfaces. For a group g, let W denote the set of all internal nodes in J having child leaf nodes in g. The fields of g do not have the same parent if and only if $|W|>1$. Let $v, u \in W$. There are two cases: (i) v and u are involved in an ancestor-descendant relationship and (ii) v and u are not in an ancestor-descendant relationship.

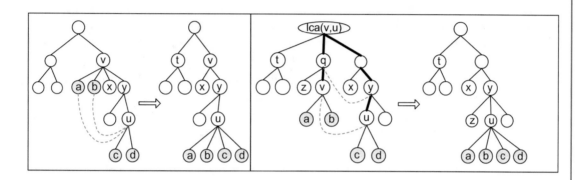

Figure 6.6: Illustrating two post processing operations.

In case (i), the algorithm simply deletes the leaf nodes of v that belong to g and makes them child nodes of u. This is illustrated in Figure 6.6 (on the left). The leaf nodes a, b, c, and d are in the same group, but they are not placed together. $W = \{v, u\}$. Because v is an ancestor of u, a, and b are placed as child nodes of u. This transformation preserves the ancestor-descendant relationships in the tree.

In case (ii), the algorithm first finds the lowest common ancestor, w, of the two nodes. Let pv and pu be the paths from v and u, respectively, to w. Suppose pv is shorter than pu. Then in a bottom-up manner, starting from v and moving up toward w, the algorithm merges the nodes on the path pv into the nodes of path pu: it first merges v into u, then the parent of v into the parent of u, and so on and so forth. It stops just before reaching node w. This case is illustrated in Figure 6.6 (on the right). The parent of a, b (i.e., v), and that of c, d (i.e., u) do not have an ancestor-descendant relationship. The nodes on the paths from v and u are merged to their lowest common ancestor (drawn with a thicker line in Figure 6.6). It first merges v and u, followed by q and y, then it stops since the parent of q is the lowest common ancestor of v and u. The rightmost tree in Figure 6.6 shows the resulting schema tree. This transformation also preserves the ancestor-descendant relationships in the tree.

J may need one final post processing operation. For each pair of nodes, v and w, with v the parent of w, if w has at most one child node, the algorithm collapses v and w into one node. After all these changes are applied to J, the resulting GQI satisfies the ancestor-descendant relationships and the grouping constraints as much as possible.

A problem specific to merging query interfaces is that the GQI may have too many fields to be user-friendly. To remedy this problem fields that are less important (e.g., they can be detected by frequencies of occurrence in the schema trees in *LQI*) can be trimmed from the GQI.

6.3   LABELING INTEGRATED QUERY INTERFACES

As it can be observed from the query interface in Figure 2.1, between the labels of the fields in the same group there are certain lexical relationships. For instance, *Adult*, *Senior*, and *Child* all are singular nouns. It is challenging to enforce such lexical uniformity among the labels of a group of fields in the GQI, because the fields may originate from several (independently designed) local query interfaces. That is, a group of fields within the GQI may not correspond to any group of fields in a single interface, making difficult the task of uniform assignment of labels to these fields. For example, consider that the global query interface is just as the one shown in Figure 2.1, but it has an additional field next to "Child," namely, a field denoting the "infants" whose label can be drawn from among "Infant," "Infants," and "Number of Infants." Clearly, the best label for this field is "Infant," since it preserves the existing lexical homogeneity (i.e., all singular nouns).

Automatic labeling must also consider the semantic ambiguity problem. Consider the query interface in the Job domain in Figure 6.7. For the sake of this example suppose the integrated interface of this domain is as shown in the figure except for an additional field denoting job preferences, i.e., part-time, full-time, etc, whose label needs to be selected from among "Job Type," "Type of Job," and "Job Preferences." Here the first two labels would not be appropriate, since they are essentially the same as another field "Job Type."

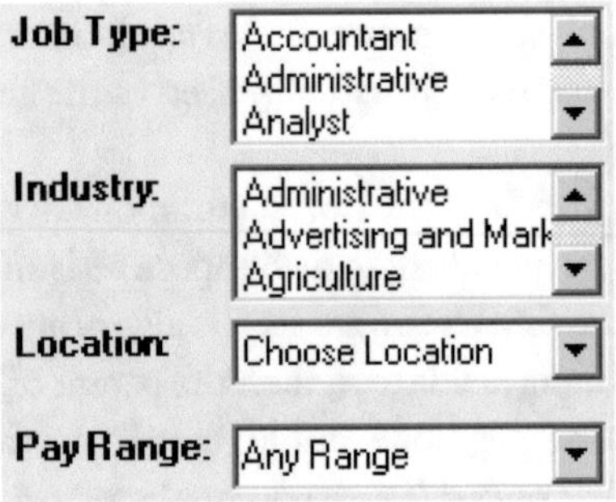

Figure 6.7: A query interface in the job search domain.

In labeling a GQI, we look to emulate the labeling of local query interfaces. It was empirically observed that field labels of local query interfaces obey certain lexical properties. First, the labels of the fields of a group are "compatible" (they resemble certain lexical homogeneity). For example, {"Adults," "Seniors," "Children"} are compatible, while {"Adults," "Seniors," "Number of Children"} are not. This property is called *horizontal consistency*. Second, the label of an internal node (i.e., a section of the query interface) is characterized by its set of descendant leaf nodes (i.e., the fields in that section). Since the set of descendant leaf nodes of an internal node v contains the set of descendant leaf nodes of any of its descendant internal nodes (i.e., subsections), w, the label of v is *semantically at least as general as* that of w. This is called *vertical consistency*. Third, the label of each internal node is "compatible" with the labels of its descendant leaf nodes. The problem is to assign labels to the (leaf and internal) nodes of a GQI from the set of labels of local query interfaces such that these three properties are preserved, if possible.

Throughout this section, we use primarily examples from the Credit Card Application domain because it has more "expressive" labels. The running example of this section is depicted in Figure 6.8. It consists of three (fragments of) query interfaces. Their corresponding GQI is also shown in the figure.

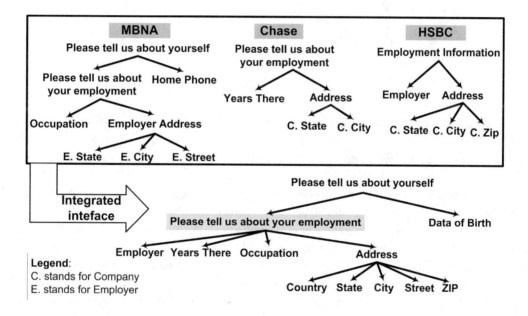

Figure 6.8: Example of four (fragments of) query interfaces in the credit card domain.

6.3.1   SEMANTIC RULES ON NAMES

The main objects manipulated in the labeling problem are the labels of the local query interfaces. The labels are treated as sets of *content words*. For example, {"provide," "financial," "information"} corresponds to the label "Please provide us with some financial information." We define three semantic relationships between labels: *equality*, *synonymy*, and *hypernymy*. They are defined using the semantic relationships among the tokens of the labels as given by WordNet [Fellbaum, 1998].

Definition 6.2   Let A and B be two labels. Let $A_{cw} = \{a_1, \ldots, a_n\}$ and $B_{cw} = \{b_1, \ldots, b_m\}$ be their sets of content words, respectively. We define the following relationships between A and B:

A *synonym* B, if there exists a bijective function $f : A_{cw} \to B_{cw}$, with $f(a) = b$, if a is either the same as or synonymous with b, where synonymy between a and b is given by WordNet.

A *hypernym* B, if there exists an injective function $g : A_{cw} \to B_{cw}$ with $f(a) = b$ if *a rel b*, where *rel* is either *identity*, *synonymy*, or *hypernymy* by WordNet. If $n = m$, then at least one *rel* is hypernymy by WordNet.

A *hyponym* B if *B hypernym A*.

Example 6.3   "Area of Study" *synonym* "Field of Work" since "area" is a synonym of "field" and "study" is a synonym of "work," by WordNet. "Financial Information" is a hypernym of "Household Financial Information." "Employment Information" is a hypernym of "Job Information," because "Employment" is a hypernym of "Job."

We sometime say that A is *string equal* to B, if A is identical to B. We may also say that A *equals* B, if $A_{cw} = B_{cw}$. For example, "Type of Job" equals "Job Type."

Labels require substantial cleaning effort. A common operation is to strip them out of attached comments and non-alphanumeric characters (e.g., the label "Date of Birth (mmddyy); no dashes or slashes" becomes "Date of Birth" after cleaning). We also need to remove the so-called stop words from labels. Consider the labels "Where do you want to go?" and "When do you want to travel?" The words "do," "to," "when," "where," and "you" are commonly regarded as not conveying any significant semantics to the texts or phrases they appear in. Consequently, they are discarded. These words are called *stop words*. The former label becomes "want go" and the latter label becomes "want travel" after the removal of the stop words from the two labels. Given that "go" and "travel" are synonyms by WordNet [16], one may infer that "want go" is semantically equivalent to "want travel." Thus, one wrongly deduces that the original labels are semantically equivalent as well. The example illustrates that there are instances when stop words express important semantic information and thus, they need to be carefully considered before removal. Their careless removal may lead to erroneous logic inferences. The problem of identifying the correct stop words in a given application domain is an NP-hard problem [Dragut et al., 2009b]. The same work also gives a heuristic-based algorithm, which we do not cover here.

6.3.2   LABELING CONSISTENCY FOR GROUPS – HORIZONTAL CONSISTENCY

Consider a group g in G with n fields. We create a relation gR for g. gR has *n+1 columns*: a column for each field in the group, plus a column for the names/ids of the query interfaces in *LQI*. A tuple (of labels) in this relation denotes the labels a query interface supplies for the fields of the group. A tuple may have null entries, because an interface may not have all the fields in the group. The set of non-null labels in a tuple represents a *consistent set of labels*. Each interface contributes at most one tuple to gR. We use the interface name to refer to a tuple in gR.

Table 6.2: An Example of Group Relation

Interface	eState	eCity	eStreet	eZipCode
HSBC	Company State	Company City		Company Zip
MBNA	Employer State	Employer City		
Chase	Company State	Company City		
NCL	Company State	Company City	Company Street	
Discover	Employer State	Employer City	Employer Street	

Table 6.2 shows such a relation. The tuple Chase provides labels for the fields eState and eCity, but not for the fields eStreet and eZipCode. The labels "Company State" and "Company City" in the tuple Chase constitute a set of consistent labels.

In practice, a query interface (i.e., a tuple) rarely supplies the labels of all the fields of a group. Consequently, we need a systematic procedure to construct a labeling solution for the group by combining multiple tuples of consistent labels. A labeling solution for the group is a new tuple with the property that its labels are consistent and it has a label for each column (element). Two tuples of labels t and s are combined if they meet one of the three levels of *inter-tuple labeling compatibility*:

String level: s and t are string compatible if $s.A$ *string equal* $t.A$ for some non-null column A of gR.

Equality level: s and t are equality compatible if $s.A$ *equal* $t.A$ for some non-null column A of gR.

Synonymy level: s and t are synonymy compatible if $s.A$ is a synonym of $t.A$ for some non-null column A of gR.

For example, in Table 6.2 the tuples HSBC, NCL, and Chase are in the string level of compatibility, whereas the tuples HSBC and MBNA do not satisfy any of the three compatibility levels.

String level is the strongest of the three: a labeling solution for a group computed in its terms should give the "most" consistent solution for the group. While the strongest in terms of its potential to find a "best" possible consistent solution, it is the most restrictive in terms of its applicability. One study showed that the probability of two subjects picking the same term for a given entity ranged from 7% to 18% [Furnas et al., 1987]. The other levels of compatibility are introduced to deal with the inherent heterogeneity of labels in the deep Web.

Mathematically, if T is the set of all tuples of labels in gR, then each level of inter-tuple labeling compatibility is a binary relation on T. If we denote by R_{str}, R_{eq}, and R_{syn}, respectively, the relations introduced by the three levels of compatibility, we have $R_{str} \subseteq R_{eq} \subseteq R_{syn}$. Let $\overline{R}_{str}$, $\overline{R}_{eq}$ and $\overline{R}_{syn}$ be the transitive closures of R_{str}, R_{eq}, and R_{syn}, respectively. The *transitive closure* of a binary relation R on a set X is the minimal transitive relation R' on X that contains R. Thus, $a R' b$ for any fields a and b of X provided that there exist $x_1, x_2, \ldots, x_n$ with $x_1 = a$, $x_n = b$ and $x_i R x_{i+1}$ for all $1 \leq i \leq n$. We may say that b is *reachable* from a. Because, R_{str}, R_{eq}, and R_{syn} are *reflexive* and *symmetric* relations, it follows that the reachability relation induced by either of them is an *equivalent* relation. Therefore, $\overline{R}_{str}$ ($\overline{R}_{eq}$ and $\overline{R}_{syn}$) partitions T into classes (subsets) of reachable tuples. That is, if $Y \subseteq T$ is a part of the partition induced by $\overline{R}_{str}$ ($\overline{R}_{eq}$ or $\overline{R}_{syn}$) on T, then for any $s, t \in T$, t is reachable from s, and vice versa. For instance, $\overline{R}_{str}$ partitions the set of tuples in Table 6.2 into two subsets (parts): {HSBC, Chase, NCL} and {MBNA, Discover}.

The algorithm for computing a consistent labeling solution for a group proceeds along the three compatibility levels as follows. First, we compute the transitive closure of R_{str}. If a solution can be obtained from the tuples in $\overline{R}_{str}$ then the algorithm stops and reports the consistent labeling solution. Else, it computes the transitive closure of R_{eq}. We check the existence of a consistent solution in $\overline{R}_{eq}$. If one cannot be computed the algorithm computes $\overline{R}_{syn}$. If a consistent labeling solution for the group cannot be derived from the tuples in $\overline{R}_{syn}$ the algorithm identifies the subset of fields of the group for which consistent labeling solutions can be constructed. The algorithm constructs the labeling solution for the group by concatenating the labeling solutions for the subsets of fields. The details are given below.

Find Labeling Consistent Fields in a Group

The ideal situation is when we can find a consistent labeling solution for the entire set of fields of a group. In general, this may not be possible; hence, we need to determine the subsets of fields of the group for which a consistent labeling can be constructed.

Let R be one of R_{str}, R_{eq}, or R_{syn}. R partitions the set of tuples T into subsets of reachable tuples. Let $Y \subseteq T$ be a part of the partition (e.g., $Y = $ {HSBC, Chase, NCL}). The tuples in Y supply a consistent solution for g if for each column A of the group relation gR there exists a tuple

$t \in Y$ such that $t.A \neq null$. That is, there is a subset of tuples in Y, when combined together gives a new tuple that has a value (label) in each column of gR.

In general, the tuples in Y may be combined in many ways, leading to multiple distinct consistent solutions for g. Various criteria can be chosen to identify the "best" solution. One criterion is the *tuple labeling expressiveness*. The expressiveness of a tuple is defined as the number of distinct content words of its constituent labels.

Interface	eNumConnections	eTicketClass	eAirline
SAS	NonStop		Choose an Airline
Airfare	Number of Connections		Airline Preference
Alldest		Class of Ticket	Preferred Airline
Cheap	Max. Number of Stops		Airline Preference
MSN		Airline	Preference

Table 6.3: Example of Inter-tuple Compatibility

Consider the group relation in Table 6.3. Suppose that the tuples of the relation are partitioned in three disjoint subsets {SAS}, {Airfare Alldest, Cheap}, and {MSN}. This set of partitions is obtained if only the first two levels of compatibility are used. Since the second partition comprises all the fields of the group, a consistent solution can be extracted. Assume that two tuple-solutions were generated: ("Max. Number of Stops," "Class of Ticket," "Preferred Airline") and ("Number of Connections," "Class of Ticket," "Airline Preference"). Employing the expressiveness criterion the former will be preferred over the latter since it has more distinct content words.

We identify all the parts of the partition similar to Y and derive a (potential) labeling solution for the group g from each of them. The selection of a final labeling solution for g from the set of all possible solutions is deferred as the solution needs to be correlated with the labels of the internal nodes of the schema tree. This is accomplished in a later stage, which will be shortly presented.

If there are no partitions similar to Y, a partially consistent labeling solution for g needs to be created. This aspect is not covered here. Interested readers are referred to the work by Dragut et al. [2006b].

6.3.3   LABELING INTERNAL NODES—VERTICAL CONSISTENCY

The process of assigning consistent labels to the internal nodes of a GQI is based on the following hypothesis: a label l is suitable for an internal node v if its semantic meaning is "rich enough" to encompass the semantic meaning of each of v's descendent leaf nodes (fields) and it is not "rich enough" to encompass the semantics of other leaf nodes. This is accomplished by introducing the concept of the set of fields (leaf nodes) *semantically covered by* a label, which will be shortly defined.

Two main resources are explored to discover meaningful labels for the internal nodes of a GQI: (i) the linguistic semantic relationships (Definition 6.2) between the labels across query interfaces and (ii) the relationship among labels induced by the ancestor-descendant relationships between internal nodes within a schema tree.

We start by illustrating the use of the linguistic semantic relationship. We show the general line of logic to infer that the label "Address" is suitable to the internal node of the integrated interface in Figure 6.8. The label "Address" appears in both interfaces Chase and HSBC. In the former it is the label of the parent node of the fields Company State and Company City, while in the latter it is the label of the parent node of the fields Company City and Company Zip. Since "Address" *string equals* "Address," we conclude that its semantics is "rich enough" to encompass all these fields, i.e., {Company State, Company City, Company Zip}. Furthermore, "Address" is a hypernym of the label "Employer Address." Hence, we infer that the semantics of "Address" also encompasses the set of descendant fields of the node labeled "Employer Address" in the interface MBNA. Consequently, "Address" *semantically covers* {Company State, Company City, Company Street, Company ZIP}. The linguistic relationships between labels are used twice in this example. We now illustrate how the ancestor-descendant relationship between labels is taken into consideration in the labeling process. The label "Please tell us about your employment" is assigned to an ancestor of the node labeled "Address" in the local interface Chase. As a result, the former label can be deemed to be *semantically more general* than the latter label because the designer of this interface through this assignment made this relationship explicit. Thus, the semantics of the label "Please tell us about your employment" should encompass the set of fields we determined for "Address" above.

Let l be a label of an internal node v in some query interface J in LQI. Denote by SC_n the set of all leaf nodes in LQI that l semantically covers. By default, SC_n contains the set of descendant leaf nodes of v in J. Suppose that SC_n is known. Then, the label l is a candidate label for an internal node v in the schema tree of the GQI if and only if $SC_n = L_v$, where L_v is the set of descendant leaf nodes of v in the schema tree. Therefore, the problem is that of computing for each label l the set of all leaf nodes that l semantically covers in LQI.

The algorithm for computing the sets of leaf nodes that the labels of the internal nodes of the query interfaces in LQI semantically cover is sketched in Figure 6.9. The algorithm iterates over the set of query interfaces until the set of leaf nodes covered by each label does not change. Two names from two distinct schema trees are compared using Definition 6.2. If they are synonyms then their sets are updated. If one of the labels is a hypernym of the other then only the context of the former label is updated.

Algorithm: Compute semantic covers for labels
Input: LQI - the set of schema trees
Output: the set of leaf nodes semantically covered by each label in LQI
repeat
    Let J_1 and J_2 be two interfaces in LQI;
    Let v be an internal node in J_1 with label l;
    Let w be an internal node in J_2 with label p;
    if l synonym p **then**
$$SC_l, SC_p \leftarrow SC_l \cup SC_p;$$
    else if l hypernym p **then**
$$SC_l \leftarrow SC_l \cup SC_p;$$
    else if p hypernym l **then**
$$SC_p \leftarrow SC_l \cup SC_p;$$
until no changes

Figure 6.9: The algorithm that computes the sets of leaf notes covered by the labels in LQI.

As in the case of groups, we do not yet choose a definite label for an internal node of a GQI. Instead, a set of candidate labels is assigned to each internal node. One of the candidate labels of an internal node is eventually selected such that the label is "compatible" with the labels of the descendant leaf nodes of the node in GQI.

A label l is *semantically at least as general as* a label l' if $SC_{l'} \subseteq SC_l$. The above method guarantees that the GQI has a *vertically consistent labeling* with respect to this definition. That is, for any two internal nodes v and w in GQI, with v an ancestor of w, the label assigned to v is semantically at least as general as that assigned to w.

6.3.4   CONSISTENT LABELED INTEGRATED INTERFACE

Now the horizontal and vertical labeling consistencies need to be combined to ensure the consistency for the entire integrated interface. In other words, the labels of the internal nodes need to be constrained to be compatible with those assigned to the leaf nodes in a GQI. Let v be an internal node in the GQI and l_v one of its candidate labels. Let g be a group of fields, such that the fields of g are descendant leaf nodes of v. Let Y be a set of tuples of labels supplying a consistent solution for g. The label l_v is compatible with the labeling solution obtained from Y if there exists a tuple t in Y such that t and l_v appear in some query interface in QI.

For example, the label "Address" of the integrated interface in Figure 6.8 is compatible with the solution {"Company State," "Company City," "Company Street," "Company Zip"} of the group in Table 6.2 derived from the set of tuples {Chase, HSBC, NCL}, because the tuple ("Company State," "Company City," null, null) and "Address" appear together in the interface Chase. The label "Please tell us about yourself" is not consistent with the labeling solution of the group since it belongs to MBNA (Figure 6.8) and MBNA is not in {Chase, HSBC, NCL}.

An integrated schema tree is *weakly consistently labeled* if it has both vertically and horizontally consistent labeling. It is *consistently labeled* if it is (1) weakly consistent labeled and (2) the labels of the internal nodes and those of the (groups of) leaf nodes are compatible.

We assume that the integrated query interface has a weakly consistent labeling solution and we present a mechanism to construct a consistently labeling solution, if one exists. For ease of exposition the following assumptions are made without loss of generality:

Each internal node has a nonempty set of candidate labels.

Each group has at least one consistent labeling solution.

Each group of leaf nodes is regarded as a mere leaf node, called *group node*.

The example depicted in Figure 6.10 illustrates the multiple facets of the problem. g, h, k denote three group nodes and next to each of them are the labeling solutions for their leaf nodes. For instance Sh_1, Sh_2, and Sh_3 are the labeling solutions of the group h. The (fragment) schema tree has three internal nodes, t, v, and w. Next to each node is its set of candidate labels. For instance, the candidate labels of node w are $L_w =$ {"Address," "Employer Address"}. The various lines from a candidate label of a node to a candidate labeling solution for a group marks that the two are compatible. For example, the label "Please tell us about your employment" of node v is consistent with the solutions Sg_1 and Sg_2 of the group g and the solution Sh_2 of the group h. Observe that no label of any internal node is consistent with Sh_1 (colored in gray). Also, the label "So, please tell us about yourself" (underlined in the figure) of the node v is not consistent with any labeling solution of any group. Hence, it is disregarded. The label "Applicant information" of the node t is also disregarded since it is only consistent with Sk_1; it is not consistent with any of the labeling solutions of g and h.

For this (fragment of) integrated schema tree there exists an assignment of labels that gives an overall consistent solution. A consistent solution is enabled by the assignment of the labels Sk_2, Sg_1, and Sh_2 to the group nodes k, g, and h, respectively. It is easy to check that each internal node has at least one candidate label consistent with this assignment. For example, the node t has label "Please tell us about yourself," the node v has label "Please tell us about your employment," and the node w has label "Company Address." On the other hand, if we assign Sk_2, Sg_1, and Sh_3 to the group nodes k, g, and h, respectively, we cannot reach a consistent solution for the entire schema tree, because the nodes t and v have no candidate labels consistent with the labeling solution Sh_3 of the group node h. This example suggests that the consistency problem for the entire schema tree reduces to finding, among all possible combinations of label assignments for the group nodes (i.e., the cross product),

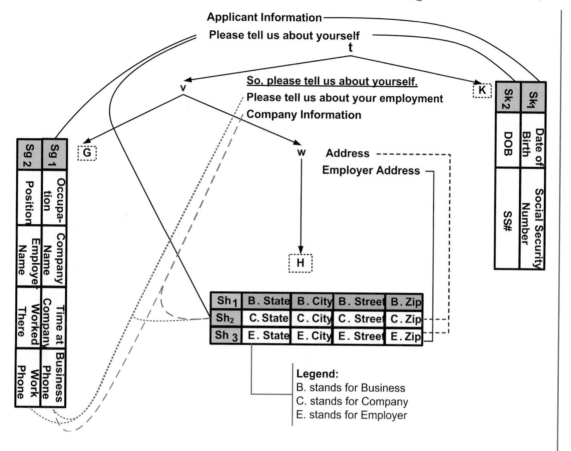

Figure 6.10: Example of all around consistency.

the one ensuring that each internal node has at least one candidate solution which is consistent with this assignment. In other words, the labels of the internal nodes act as constraints on the set of all possible label assignments for the groups nodes. It can be shown that the consistent labeling problem of a GQI is an instance of the well known *constraint satisfaction problem* (CSP) [Dechter, 2003].

While the CSP is an intractable problem, the problem of consistently labeling an integrated interface has a polynomial algorithm. The input of the algorithm is the schema tree of a GQI with a weak labeling consistent solution. The output is the set of possible assignments to the group nodes that make the entire interface consistently labeled. The algorithm follows a bottom-up traversal strategy that for each internal node v, tests if the intersection between the set of constraints of v and the set of constraints satisfied in each of the subtrees rooted at the child nodes of v is nonempty. If the intersection is not empty when the root is reached, then GQI has a consistent labeling solution. Otherwise, it has no consistent labeling solution. More details are given by Dragut [2010].

CHAPTER 7

Summary and Future Research

Many Web applications and systems, such as deep Web crawling/surfacing and Web database integration systems, need to interact with the query interfaces of deep Web data sources. To support these applications, techniques are needed to extract such query interfaces and analyze them. In the context of building Web database integration systems or database metasearch engines, additional techniques are needed to cluster query interfaces according to their domains, to match attributes/fields across different query interfaces in the same domain, and to integrate the query interfaces in the same domain into an integrated query interface. Furthermore, due to the existence of a very large number of Web databases (tens of millions) and their fast changing nature, it is essential that the above mentioned techniques be highly automated so that human involvement can be minimized.

This book is an attempt to provide a comprehensive and in-depth review of the state-of-the-art techniques involving different aspects of processing deep Web query interfaces that have been developed over the last 10 years. The specific topics that were covered in this book include query interface modeling, query interface extraction, query interface clustering, attribute matching across different query interfaces, attribute integration, and query interface integration. These topics were presented in the context of automatically constructing a high-quality integrated query interface for the query interfaces in each domain. The integrated query interface for a domain is to be used as the query interface of the Web database integration system over the many Web databases in the domain. Although it is not the objective of this book to cover the techniques for building Web database integration systems, the key components of such systems are outlined early in the book to provide the appropriate context for the main contents of this book.

The process of generating integrated query interfaces for local query interfaces in different domains starts with developing an interface schema model to represent the schema information in each query interface. Two types of interface schema models were presented in Chapter 2 of this book – a flat model and a hierarchical model, with the latter capturing additional relationships among the search fields, namely ordering and ancestor-descendant relationships. The process continues with employing techniques to extract the interface schema information from each interface page. Both techniques that perform interface extraction from the HTML source code of the search form directly and those that also utilize visual information on rendered interface pages were covered in Chapter 2. The next step of the process groups query interfaces by their domains. Both clustering and categorization solutions for performing this grouping were introduced in Chapter 3. The process then continues with identifying matching attributes/fields across different query interfaces in the same domain. Techniques that exploit a variety of information such as information at label/name level, schema level (i.e., metadata level), and value level were discussed in Chapter 4 of this book.

With matching attributes across local query interfaces identified, the process moves to integrate the local query interfaces into a single unified interface. This step was covered in two chapters in this book. First, techniques for integrating matching attributes were presented in Chapter 5; they include techniques for determining the label, domain type, and external values (both non-numerical and numerical, including ranges) of each global attribute. Second, other aspects of integrating multiple query interfaces based on the hierarchical interface schema model were covered in Chapter 6 and they include trying to retain the ordering of sibling fields and the ancestor-descendant relationships from local interfaces as much as possible, and generating a global schema with consistent labels for all fields in the same group and between ancestor and descendant nodes in the hierarchy. As query interface integration has its root in database schema integration, a brief review of relevant issues in database schema integration was also provided in each chapter of the book.

Deep Web query interface has been a subject of extensive research in the last 10 years. As reviewed in this book, many issues related to these interfaces have been investigated and much progress has been made. However, there are still a number of significant issues in this area that either have not been addressed or have not been adequately addressed. Some of these issues are described below.

Integration of constraints. As discussed in Chapter 2, an attribute may consist of two types of fields; domain fields and constraint fields. When multiple matching local attributes have constraint fields, there is a need to integrate them for the integrated global attribute. To the best of our knowledge, this problem has not been seriously investigated before. There are several issues in this problem. First, the semantic of each constraint needs to be understood. Second, relationships among constraints from different interfaces need to be identified. Two constraints from two interfaces may be independent, equivalent, one is subsumed by the other, and conflicting. Our observation shows that constraints are usually implemented as radio buttons and checkboxes, and usually at most one constraint is used for each query. Therefore, it is acceptable to have conflicting constraint fields for the same attribute. Third, decide what constraint(s) to use for the global attributes. Note that if a constraint is not supported by a local attribute, the condition of the constraint needs to be evaluated by the global system after the data from the local system are retrieved.

Integration of attribute values. The issue of integrating the external values of multiple matching attributes was discussed in significant detail in Chapter 5. Nonetheless, this is an under researched issue. The discussions in Chapter 5 show that the choice of using more generic or more specific values (for range values, using wider or narrow ranges) has a significant impact on the efficiency of the Web database integration system when it is used to evaluate user queries. However, beyond a small study [Jiang et al., 2008], there is little published work in examining this issue more systematically and in evaluating the performance of different choices using large-scale datasets.

Extraction and understanding of dynamic query interfaces. An increasing number of query interfaces are dynamic in the sense that the query interface may alter after certain fields are selected. Two types of dynamic changes have been observed. The first is the change of values of some fields (e.g., values under a selection list). For example, for the query interface at `http://www.cars.com`[8], after a value for the field *Make* is selected, the values of the field *Model* change automatically so that the values are models of the selected make. The second is the structure of the query interface (e.g., some fields are added, deleted, or modified). For example, for the query interface at `http://www.expedia.com`[9], when the radio button "One way" is selected, the set of fields in the query interface is changed to match this selection (i.e., fields pertinent to *Returning Time* are removed). The current query interface models do not consider dynamic query interfaces and they need to be extended to capture the dynamic aspect of these interfaces.

Extraction and understanding of query interfaces using javascript. In recent years, an increasing number of query interfaces are no longer implemented using just the standard HTML form tag, but many also add javascript and AJAX features into the search forms. These features can make the query interfaces more dynamic and more powerful. Not only do dynamic query interfaces (see the previous item) heavily use these features, but many static query interfaces also employ them. For example, javascript is also used in the query interface at `http://www.ncbi.nlm.nih.gov`[10] as well as in the BLAST interfaces available from `http://blast.ncbi.nlm.nih.gov`[11]. The existence of javascript in search forms of query interfaces adds a significant challenge to query interface extraction and understanding. Although a technique for extracting AJAX content has been reported [Duda et al., 2009], this technique cannot handle search forms. We are not aware of any published work addressing this challenge directly.

Automatic maintenance of integrated query interfaces. It is likely that over time some existing Web databases may cease to exist and many new Web databases will be created. As a result, there is a need to delete local query interfaces from and add local query interfaces to an existing integrated interface of a given domain. This maintenance issue was briefly mentioned by He et al. [2004c] but not in the context of the multi-level hierarchical interface model. A recent work proposed a method to generate a customized query interface based on a subset of selected query interfaces from an existing query interface created based on a larger set of query interfaces [Dragut et al., 2009a] in the context of the hierarchical interface model. This method can be used to delete local query interfaces from an existing integrated query interface. But this method does not address issues concerning the addition of new query interfaces to an existing integrated query interface. There are two specific issues here: incremental maintenance

---

[8] Accessed on March 19, 2012.
[9] Accessed on March 19, 2012.
[10] Accessed on March 20, 2012.
[11] Accessed on March 20, 2012.

of semantic groups of fields and maintaining the labeling consistency of the integrated interface when new interfaces are added to a domain.

Handling boundary query interfaces in Web-scale clustering. There are two challenges in Web-scale clustering of query interfaces [Madhavan et al., 2007; Mahmoud and Aboulnaga, 2010]. One is that the number of domains is unknown in advance, which means that the number of clusters is unknown in advance. The other is that there are likely many query interfaces with unclear domains, i.e., they appear between boundaries of multiple domains. The solutions proposed by Mahmoud and Aboulnaga [2010] include using agglomerative clustering to bypass the need to know the number of clusters and allowing the same interface to be assigned to multiple clusters with an estimated probability that an interface belongs to a cluster. However, the current solutions are not sufficiently accurate and have significant room to improve. For example, only attribute names/labels are used in this solution and a significant amount of information that can be extracted from query interfaces such as external values and terms in query interface pages is not utilized. Furthermore, when new query interfaces are discovered, there is a need to perform incremental clustering to avoid re-starting the clustering from scratch, which would be very expensive for Web-scale clustering.

Evaluation of the entire query interface integration process. To build Web-scale deep Web integration systems, it is necessary to automate the entire query interface integration process. This process consists of a number of inter-related tasks, i.e., query interface extraction, query interface clustering, query interface matching, attribute integration, and query interface integration. As illustrated in this book, there has been substantial work on each of these tasks. Due to the nature of automated solutions, all proposed solutions make mistakes in some cases. Although the solutions for each task have been evaluated, there is a lack of comprehensive evaluation of the entire process. With the exception of the work by He and Chang [2005], which studies the issue of the quality of query interface extraction for query interface matching, the effect of errors in one component on the effectiveness of another component and the accumulative effect of errors in each component on the quality of the final integrated query interface have largely not been investigated but are highly desired.

Query interface understanding and integration is a significant component of the general task of building Web database integration systems. It is related to several other components of this general task, including global query evaluation, query translation (query mapping) from global queries to local queries, query dispatching (i.e., pass translated queries to local Web databases), and search result schema matching [Chuang and Chang, 2008]. Query interface integration is the embodiment of database schema integration on the Web. It is also a special case of the more general ontology integration problem. A rich resource on ontology matching and integration is available at `http://ontologymatching.org/index.html`[12].

---

[12] Accessed on March 22, 2012.

Bibliography

S. Al-Fedaghi and P. Scheuermann (1981) Mapping considerations in the design of schemas for the relational model. *IEEE Trans. Software Engineering* 7(1), 99–111.
DOI: 10.1109/TSE.1981.234512 Cited on page(s) 113

A. Arasu and H. Garcia-Molina (2003) Extracting structured data from Web pages. In *Proc. ACM SIGMOD Int. Conf. on Management of Data*, 337–348. DOI: 10.1145/872757.872799 Cited on page(s) 14

L. Barbosa and J. Freire (2004) Siphoning hidden-web data through keyword-based interfaces. In *Proc. Brazilian Symposium on Data Base*, 309–321. Cited on page(s) 11

L. Barbosa and J. Freire (2007a) Combining classifiers to identify online databases. In *Proc. 16th Int. Conf. on World Wide Web*, 431–440. DOI: 10.1145/1242572.1242631 Cited on page(s) 47, 48, 53, 65

L. Barbosa and J. Freire (2007b) An adaptive crawler for locating hidden-Web entry points. In *Proc.16th Int. Conf. on World Wide Web*, 441–450. DOI: 10.1145/1242572.1242632 Cited on page(s) 46, 47, 64

L. Barbosa, J. Freire and A. Silva (2007) Organizing hidden-Web databases by clustering visible Web documents. In *Proc. IEEE Int. Conf. on Data Engineering*, 326–335. Cited on page(s) 53, 60

C. Batini and M. Lenzerini (1984) A methodology for data schema integration in the entity-relationship model. *IEEE Trans. on Software Engineering* 10(6), 650–664.
DOI: 10.1109/TSE.1984.5010294 Cited on page(s) 113

C. Batini, M. Lenzerini and S. Navathe (1984) A comparative analysis of methodologies for database schema integration. *ACM Computing Surveys* 18(4), 323–364. DOI: 10.1145/27633.27634 Cited on page(s) 70

Z. Bellahsene, A. Bonifati and E. Rahm (Eds.) (2011) *Schema Matching and Mapping*. Springer.
DOI: 10.1007/978-3-642-16518-4 Cited on page(s) 70

A. Bergholz and B. Chidlovskii (2003) Crawling for domain-specific hidden Web resources. In *Proc. Int. Conf. on Web Information System Engineering*, 125–133. DOI: 10.1109/WISE.2003.1254476 Cited on page(s) 31, 46

M. Bergman (2001) White paper: The deep web: Surfacing the hidden value. *The Journal of Electronic Publishing* 7(1), August. DOI: 10.3998/3336451.0007.104 Cited on page(s) 2

K. S. Booth and G. S. Lueker (1976) Testing for the consecutive ones property, interval graphs, and graph planarity using PQ-tree algorithms. *J. Comput. Syst. Sci.* 13(3):335–379. DOI: 10.1016/S0022-0000(76)80045-1 Cited on page(s) 118

A. Broder, R. Kumar, F. Maghoul, P. Raghavan, S. Rajagopalan, R. Stata, A. Tomkins and J. Wiener (2000) Graph structure in the Web. In *Proc. Int. World Wide Web Conf.*, 309–320. DOI: 10.1016/S1389-1286(00)00083-9 Cited on page(s) 3

D. Buttler, L. Liu and C. Pu (2001) A fully automated object extraction system for the World Wide Web. In *Proc. 21st Int. Conf. on Distributed Computing Systems*, paper 361. DOI: 10.1109/ICDSC.2001.918966 Cited on page(s) 14

M. J. Cafarella, E. Chang, A. Fikes, A. Halevy, W. Hsieh, A. Lerner, J. Madhavan and S. Muthukrishnan (2008) Data management projects at Google. *ACM SIGMOD Record* 37(1), 34–38. DOI: 10.1145/1374780.1374789 Cited on page(s) 3, 26

M. J. Cafarella, A. Halevy and J. Madhavan (2011) Structured data on the Web. *Commun. ACM* 54(2), 72–79. DOI: 10.1145/1897816.1897839 Cited on page(s) 2, 15

G. Casella and R. L. Berger (2001) *Statistical Inference*. Duxbury Press, 2nd ed. Cited on page(s) 56, 58, 86

S. Chakrabarti, M. van den Berg and B. Dom (1999) Focused crawling: A new approach to topic-specific Web resource discovery. In *Proc. 8th Int. Conf. World Wide Web*, 1623–1640. DOI: 10.1016/S1389-1286(99)00052-3 Cited on page(s) 46

K. C.-C. Chang, B. He, C. Li, M. Patel and Z. Zhang (2004) Structured databases on the Web: Observations and implications. *ACM SIGMOD Record* 33(3), 61–70. DOI: 10.1145/1031570.1031584 Cited on page(s) 28

K. C.-C. Chang, B. He and Z. Zhang (2005) Toward large scale integration: Building a MetaQuerier over databases on the Web. In *Proc. 2nd Conf. on Innovative Data Systems Research*, 44–55. Cited on page(s) 37

C. H. Chang, M. Kayed, M. R. Girgis and K. F. Shaalan (2006) A survey of Web information extraction systems. *IEEE Trans. Knowl. and Data Eng.* 18(10), 1411–1428. DOI: 10.1109/TKDE.2006.152 Cited on page(s) 14, 91

S.-L. Chuang and K. C.-C. Chang (2008) Integrating Web query results: Holistic schema matching. In *Proc. 17th ACM Conf. on Information and Knowledge Management*, 33–42. DOI: 10.1145/1458082.1458090 Cited on page(s) 91, 138

J. Cope, N. Craswell and D. Hawking (2003) Automated discovery of search interfaces on the Web. In *Proc. 14th Australasian Database Conf.*, 181–189. Cited on page(s) 11

V. Crescenzi, G. Mecca and P. Merialdo (2001) RoadRunner: Towards automatic data extraction from large Web sites. In *Proc. 27th Int. Conf. on Very Large Data Bases*, 109–118. Cited on page(s) 14

A. Dasgupta, X. Jin, B. Jewell, N. Zhang and G. Das (2010) Unbiased estimation of size and other aggregates over hidden Web databases. In *Proc. ACM SIGMOD Int. Conf. on Management of Data*, 855–866. DOI: 10.1145/1807167.1807259 Cited on page(s) 46

R. Dechter (2003) *Constraint Processing*. Morgan Kaufmann Publishers. Cited on page(s) 133

R. Dhamankar, Y. Lee, A. Doan, A. Halevy and P. Domingos (2004) iMAP: Discovering complex semantic matches between database schemas. In *Proc. ACM SIGMOD Int. Conf. on Management of Data*, 383–394. DOI: 10.1145/1007568.1007612 Cited on page(s) 18

E. C. Dragut (2010) *A Framework for Transparently Accessing Deep Web Sources*. Ph.D. Thesis, Department of Computer Science, University of Illinois at Chicago, Chicago, Illinois. Cited on page(s) 133

E. C. Dragut, W. Wu, P. Sistla, C. Yu and W. Meng (2006a) Merging source query interfaces on Web databases. In *Proc. 22nd Int. Conf. on Data Engineering*, 679–690. DOI: 10.1109/ICDE.2006.91 Cited on page(s) 111, 116, 119

E. C. Dragut, C. Yu and W. Meng (2006b) Meaningful labeling of integrated query interfaces. In *Proc. 32nd Int. Conf. on Very Large Data Bases*, 679–690. Cited on page(s) 111, 129

E. C. Dragut, F. Fang, C. Yu and W. Meng (2009a) Deriving customized integrated Web query interfaces. In *Proc. IEEE/WIC/ACM Int. Joint Conf. on Web Intelligence and Intelligent Agent Technology*, 685–688. DOI: 10.1109/WI-IAT.2009.115 Cited on page(s) 137

E. C. Dragut, F. Fang, P. Sistla, C. Yu and W. Meng (2009b) Stop word and related problems in web interface integration. *Proc. VLDB Endow.* 2(1), 349–360. Cited on page(s) 28, 74, 121, 126

E. C. Dragut, T. Kabisch, C. Yu and U. Leser (2009c) A hierarchical approach to model web query interfaces for web source integration. *Proc. VLDB Endow.* 2(1), 325–336. Cited on page(s) 12, 23, 26, 29, 30, 32, 33

C. Duda, G. Frey, D. Kossmann, R. Matter and C. Zhou (2009) AJAX crawl: Making AJAX applications searchable. In *Proc. IEEE Int. Conf. Data Engineering*, 78–89. DOI: 10.1109/ICDE.2009.90 Cited on page(s) 137

A. K. Elmagarmid, P. G. Ipeirotis and V. S. Verykios (2007) Duplicate record detection: A survey. *IEEE Trans. Knowl. and Data Eng.* 19(1), 1–16. DOI: 10.1109/TKDE.2007.250581 Cited on page(s) 19

D. W. Embley, Y. Jiang and Y.-K. Ng (1999) Record-boundary discovery in Web-documents. In *Proc. ACM SIGMOD Int. Conf. on Management of Data*, 467–478. DOI: 10.1145/304181.304223 Cited on page(s) 15

W. Fang, Z. Cui and P. Zhao (2007) Ontology-based focused crawling of deep web sources. In *Proc. 2nd Int. Conf. on Knowledge Science, Engineering and Management*, 514–519. DOI: 10.1007/978-3-540-76719-0_51 Cited on page(s) 31, 46

C. Fellbaum (1998) *WordNet: An Electronic Lexical Database*. MIT Press. Cited on page(s) 73, 75, 99, 126

T. Furche, G. Gottlob, G. Grasso, X. Guo, G. Orsi and C. Schallhart (2011) Real understanding of real estate forms. In *Proc. Int. Conf. on Web Intelligence, Mining and Semantics*, paper 13. DOI: 10.1145/1988688.1988704 Cited on page(s) 30, 32, 37

G. W. Furnas, T. K. Landauer, L. M. Gomez and S. T. Dumais (1987) The vocabulary problem in human-system communication. *Commun. ACM* 30(11), 964–971. DOI: 10.1145/32206.32212 Cited on page(s) 128

A. Gal (2011) *Uncertain Schema Matching*. Morgan and Claypool. DOI: 10.2200/S00337ED1V01Y201102DTM013 Cited on page(s) 76

M. Galperin (2005) The molecular biology database collection: 2005 update. *Nucleic Acids Res.* 33. DOI: 10.1093/nar/gki139 Cited on page(s) 45

E. J. Golin (1991) Parsing visual languages with picture layout grammars. *J. Vis. Lang. Comput.* 2(4), 371–393. DOI: 10.1016/S1045-926X(05)80005-9 Cited on page(s) 37

B. He and K. C-C. Chang (2003) Statistical schema matching across Web query interfaces. In *Proc. ACM SIGMOD Int. Conf. on Management of Data*, 217–228. DOI: 10.1145/872757.872784 Cited on page(s) 12, 69, 77, 82, 83, 86, 87

B. He and K. C.-C. Chang (2005) Making holistic schema matching robust: An ensemble approach. In *Proc. 11th ACM SIGKDD Int. Conf. on Knowledge Discovery in Data Mining*, 429–438. DOI: 10.1145/1081870.1081920 Cited on page(s) 138

B. He and K. C.-C. Chang (2006) Automatic complex schema matching across Web query interfaces: A correlation mining approach. *ACM Trans. Database Syst.* 31(1), 346–395. DOI: 10.1145/1132863.1132872 Cited on page(s) 111, 116

H. He, W. Meng, C. Yu and Z. Wu (2003) WISE-Integrator: An automatic integrator of Web search interfaces for E-commerce. In *Proc. 29th Int. Conf. on Very Large Data Bases*, 357–368. Cited on page(s) 69, 74, 75, 81, 82, 99, 100, 101, 105, 108

B. He, K. C.-C. Chang and J. Han (2004a) Discovering complex matchings across web query interfaces: A correlation mining approach. In *Proc. 10th ACM SIGKDD Int. Conf. on Knowledge Discovery and Data Mining*, 148–157. DOI: 10.1145/1014052.1014071 Cited on page(s) 70, 82, 87, 90, 111

B. He, T. Tao and K. C.-C. Chang (2004b) Organizing structured web sources by query schemas: A clustering approach. In *Proc. 13th ACM Int. Conf. on Information and Knowledge Management*, 22–31. DOI: 10.1145/1031171.1031178 Cited on page(s) 53, 55, 56

H. He, W. Meng, C. Yu and Z. Wu (2004c) Automatic integration of Web search interfaces with WISE-Integrator. *VLDB Journal* 13(3), 256–273. DOI: 10.1007/s00778-004-0126-4 Cited on page(s) 102, 111, 137

H. He, W. Meng, C. Yu and Z. Wu (2005) WISE-Integrator: A system for extracting and integrating complex Web search interfaces of the deep Web. In *Proc. Int. Conf. on Very Large Data Bases*, 1314–1317. Cited on page(s) 33, 74

H. He, W. Meng, Y. Lu, C. Yu and Z. Wu (2007) Towards deeper understanding of the search interfaces of the deep Web. *World Wide Web Journal* 10(2), 133–155. DOI: 10.1007/s11280-006-0010-9 Cited on page(s) 12, 23, 26, 27, 30, 32, 33, 34, 36

I. F. Ilyas, G. Beskales and M. A. Solimam (2008) A Survey of top-k query processing techniques in relational database systems. *ACM Computing Surveys* 40(4), paper 11. DOI: 10.1145/1391729.1391730 Cited on page(s) 19

F. Jiang, L. Jia, W. Meng and X. Meng (2008) MrCoM: A cost model for range query translation in deep Web data integration. In *Proc. 4th Int. Conf. on Semantics, Knowledge and Grid*, 263–270. DOI: 10.1109/SKG.2008.69 Cited on page(s) 136

X. Jin, N. Zhang and G. Das (2011) Attribute domain discovery for hidden Web databases. In *Proc. ACM SIGMOD Int. Conf. on Management of Data*, Industrial track, 553–564. DOI: 10.1145/1989323.1989381 Cited on page(s) 11, 26, 46, 49

T. Kabisch, E. C. Dragut, C. Yu and U. Leser (2010) Deep web integration with VisQI. *Proc. VLDB Endow.* 3(1-2), 1613–1616. Cited on page(s) 39

G. Kabra, C. Li and K. C.-C. Chang (2005) Query routing: Finding ways in the maze of the deep Web. In *Proc. ICDE International Workshop on Challenges in Web Information Retrieval and Integration*, 64–73. DOI: 10.1109/WIRI.2005.33 Cited on page(s) 17

O. Kaljuvee, O. Buyukkokten, H. Garcia-Molina and A. Paepcke (2001) Efficient Web form entry on PDAs. In *Proc. 10th Int. Conf. on World Wide Web*, 663–672. DOI: 10.1145/371920.372180 Cited on page(s) 23, 32, 33

R. Khare and Y. An (2009) An empirical study on using hidden markov model for search inter-face segmentation. In *Proc. 18th ACM Conf. on Information and knowledge Management*, 17–26. DOI: 10.1145/1645953.1645959 Cited on page(s) 30, 32, 33

R. Khare, Y. An and I-Y. Song (2010) Understanding deep web search interfaces: A survey. *ACM SIGMOD Record* 39(1), 33–40. DOI: 10.1145/1860702.1860708 Cited on page(s) 23

W. Kim, I. Choi, S. Gala and M. Scheevel (1995) On resolving schematic heterogeneity in multi-database systems. In W. Kim, Ed., *Modern Database Systems: The Object Model, Interoperability, and Beyond*, 521–550. ACM Press. DOI: 10.1007/BF01263333 Cited on page(s) 96, 98

A. Laender, B. Ribeiro-Neto, A. da Silva and J. Teixeira (2002) A brief survey of Web data extraction tools. *ACM SIGMOD Record* 31(2), 84–93. DOI: 10.1145/565117.565137 Cited on page(s) 14

H. Q. Le and S. Conrad (2010) Classifying structured Web sources using aggressive feature selection. *Lecture Notes in Business Information Processing* 45(IV), 270–282. DOI: 10.1007/978-3-642-12436-5_20 Cited on page(s) 53, 64, 65

P. Lin, Y. Du, X. Tan and C. Lv (2008) Research on automatic classification for deep Web query interfaces. In *Proc. Int. Symp. on Information Processing*, 313–317. DOI: 10.1109/ISIP.2008.140 Cited on page(s) 53

B. Liu (2007) *Web Data Mining: Exploring Hyperlinks, Contents, and Usage Data*. Springer. Cited on page(s) 56

H. Liu, E. Milios and J. Janssen (2004) Probabilistic models for focused web crawling. In *Proc. 6th annual ACM Int. Workshop on Web Information and Data Management*, 16–22. DOI: 10.1145/1031453.1031458 Cited on page(s) 46

W. Liu, X. Meng and W. Meng (2010) ViDE: A vision-based approach for deep Web data extraction. *IEEE Trans. Knowl. and Data Eng.* 22(3), 447–460. DOI: 10.1109/TKDE.2009.109 Cited on page(s) 14

J. Liu, L. Jiang, Z. Wu and Q. Zheng (2011) Deep Web adaptive crawling based on minimum executable pattern. *J. Intel. Inf. Syst.* 36(2), 197–215. DOI: 10.1007/s10844-010-0124-5 Cited on page(s) 46

Y. Lu, H. He, Q. Peng, W. Meng and C. Yu (2006) Clustering e-commerce search engines based on their search interface pages using WISE-Cluster. *Data Knowl. Eng.* 59(2), 231–246. DOI: 10.1016/j.datak.2006.01.010 Cited on page(s) 53, 55, 60, 62, 63

Y. Lu, H. He, H. Zhao, W. Meng and C. Yu (2007) Annotating structured data of the deep Web. In *Proc. 23rd Int. Conf. on Data Engineering*, 376–385. DOI: 10.1109/ICDE.2007.367883 Cited on page(s) 15

Y. Lu, H. He, H. Zhao, W. Meng and C. Yu (2012) Annotating search results from Web databases. *IEEE Trans. Knowl. and Data Eng.* (to appear). DOI: 10.1109/TKDE.2011.175 Cited on page(s) 15

J. Madhavan, S. Cohen, X. Dong, A. Halevy, A. Jeffery, D. Ko and C. Yu (2007) Web-scale data integration: You can afford to pay as you go. In *Proc. 3rd Biennial Conf. on Innovative Data Systems Research*, 342–350. Cited on page(s) 10, 11, 20, 138

J. Madhavan, D. Ko, L. Kot, V. Ganapathy, A. Rasmussen and A. Y. Halevy (2008) Google's deep Web crawl. In *Proc. 34th Int. Conf. on Very Large Data Bases*, pages 1241–1252. DOI: 10.1145/1454159.1454163 Cited on page(s) 3, 11, 13, 15, 26, 31, 46, 49, 51, 52, 53

J. Madhavan, L. Afanasiev, L. Antova and A. Halevy (2009) Harnessing the deep web: Present and future. In *Proc. 4th Biennial Conf. on Innovative Data Systems Research*. Cited on page(s) 3

H. A. Mahmoud and A. Aboulnaga (2010) Schema clustering and retrieval for multi-domain pay-as-you-go data integration systems. In *Proc. ACM SIGMOD Int. Conf. on Management of Data*, 411–422. DOI: 10.1145/1807167.1807213 Cited on page(s) 53, 55, 60, 138

J. Meidanis, O. Porto and G. P. Telles (1998) On the consecutive ones property. *Discrete Applied Mathematics* 88(1-3), 325–354. DOI: 10.1016/S0166-218X(98)00078-X Cited on page(s) 118

W. Meng and C. Yu (1995) Query processing in multidatabase systems. In W. Kim, Ed., *Modern Database Systems: The Object Model, Interoperability, and Beyond*, 551–572. Addison-Wesley/ACM Press. Cited on page(s) 97

W. Meng and C. Yu (2010) *Advanced Metasearch Engine Technology*. Morgan and Claypool Publishers. DOI: 10.2200/S00307ED1V01Y201011DTM011 Cited on page(s) 12, 14, 16, 19

H. Nguyen, T. Nguyen and J. Freire (2008) Learning to extract form labels. *Proc. VLDB Endow.* 1(1), 684–694. DOI: 10.1145/1453856.1453931 Cited on page(s) 23, 24, 29, 32, 33

T. Nguyen, H. Nguyen and J. Freire (2010) PruSM: A prudent schema matching approach for web forms. In *Proc. 19th ACM Int. Conf. on Information and Knowledge Management*, 1385–1388. DOI: 10.1145/1871437.1871627 Cited on page(s) 70, 82

T. Nie, D. Shen, G. Yu and Y. Kou (2008) Subject-oriented classification based on scale probing in the deep Web. In *Proc. 9th Int. Conf. on Web-Age Information Management*, 224–229. DOI: 10.1109/WAIM.2008.85 Cited on page(s) 53, 63, 65

U. Noor, Z. Rashid and A. Rauf (2011) A survey of automatic deep Web classification techniques. *Int. Journal of Computer Applications* 19(6), 43–50. DOI: 10.5120/2362-3099 Cited on page(s) 53

C. Olston and M. Najork (2010) Web crawling. *Foundations and Trends in Information Retrieval* 4(3), 175–246. DOI: 10.1561/1500000017 Cited on page(s) 45, 46

C. Parent and S. Spaccapietra (1998) Issues and approaches of database integration. *Communications of the ACM* 41(5), 166–178. DOI: 10.1145/276404.276408 Cited on page(s) 70

S. Raghavan and H. Garcia-Molina (2001) Crawling the hidden Web. In *Proc. 27th Int. Conf. on Very Large Data Bases*, 129–138. Cited on page(s) 2, 11, 29, 31, 32, 33, 46, 49

E. Rahm and P. A. Bernstein (2001) A survey of approaches to automatic schema matching. *The VLDB Journal* 10, 334–350. DOI: 10.1007/s007780100057 Cited on page(s) 70, 71

S. Ram and V. Ramesh (1999) Schema integration: Past, present, and future. In A. Elmagarmid, M. Rusinkiewicz and A. Sheth, Eds., *Management of Heterogeneous and Autonomous Database Systems*, 119–155. Morgan Kaufmann Publishers. Cited on page(s) 70, 96, 113

Y. Ru and E. Horowitz (2005) Indexing the invisible Web: A survey. *Online Information Review* 29(3), 249–265. DOI: 10.1108/14684520510607579 Cited on page(s) 53

G. Salton and M. McGill (1983) *Introduction to Modern Information Retrieval*. McGraw-Hill. Cited on page(s) 51, 52, 53, 61, 75, 93

D. Shestakov, S. S. Bhowmick and E. Lim (2005) DEQUE: Querying the deep web. *Data and Knowledge Engineering* 52(3), 273–311. DOI: 10.1016/S0169-023X(04)00107-7 Cited on page(s) 29, 32, 33

A. Sheth and J. Larson (1990) Federated database systems for managing distributed, heterogeneous, and autonomous databases. *ACM Comput. Surv.* 22(3), 183–236. DOI: 10.1145/96602.96604 Cited on page(s) 70

M. Shokouhi and L. Si (2011) Federated search. *Foundations and Trends in Information Retrieval* 5(1), 1–102. DOI: 10.1561/1500000010 Cited on page(s) 16

L. Shu, W. Meng, H. He and C. Yu (2007) Querying capability modeling and construction. In *Proc. 8th International Conference on Web Information Systems Engineering*, 13–25. DOI: 10.1007/978-3-540-76993-4_2 Cited on page(s) 12

P. Shvaiko and J. Euzenat (2005) A survey of schema-based matching approaches. *Journal on Data Semantics* 4, 146–171. DOI: 10.1007/11603412_5 Cited on page(s) 70

K. Simon and G. Lausen (2005) ViPER: Augmenting automatic information extraction with visual perceptions. In *Proc. Int. Conf. on Information and Knowledge Management*, 381–388. DOI: 10.1145/1099554.1099672 Cited on page(s) 14

W. Su, J. Wang and F. Lochovsky (2006a) Holistic schema matching for web query interfaces. In *Proc. 10th Int. Conf. on Advances in Database Technology*, 77–94. DOI: 10.1007/11687238_8 Cited on page(s) 70, 83, 87, 90

W. Su, J. Wang and F. Lochovsky (2006b) Automatic hierarchical classification of structured deep Web databases. In *Proc. 7th Int. Conf. on Web Information Systems Engineering*, 210–221. DOI: 10.1007/11912873_23 Cited on page(s) 53, 64, 65, 66

W. Su, J. Wang and F. H. Lochovsky (2009) ODE: Ontology-assisted data extraction. *ACM Trans. Database Syst.* 34(2). DOI: 10.1145/1538909.1538914 Cited on page(s) 15

C. Thieme and A. Siebes (1993) Schema integration in object-oriented databases. In *Proc. 5th Int. Symp. on Advanced Information Systems Engineering*, 54–70. DOI: 10.1007/3-540-56777-1_4 Cited on page(s) 113

J. Wang and F. H. Lochovsky (2003) Data extraction and label assignment for Web databases. In *Proc. 12th Int. World Wide Web Conf.*, 187–196. DOI: 10.1145/775152.775179 Cited on page(s) 14, 15, 91

J. Wang, J. Wen, F. Lochovsky and W.-Y. Ma (2004) Instance-based schema matching for web databases by domain-specific query probing. In *Proc. 30th Int. Conf. on Very Large Data Bases*, 408–419. Cited on page(s) 31, 46, 70, 90

Y. Wang, W. Zuo, T. Peng and F. He (2008) Domain-specific deep Web sources discovery. In *Proc. 4th Int. Conf. on Natural Computation*, 202–206. DOI: 10.1109/ICNC.2008.350 Cited on page(s) 46

Y. Wang, J. Lu and J. Chen (2009) Crawling deep Web Using a new set covering algorithm. In *Proc. 5th Int. Conf. on Advanced Data Mining and Applications*, 326–337. DOI: 10.1007/978-3-642-03348-3_32 Cited on page(s)

Z. Wu, V. Raghavan, H. Qian, V. Rama K, W. Meng, H. He and C. Yu (2003) Towards automatic incorporation of search engines into a large-scale metasearch engine. In *Proc. IEEE/WIC Int. Conf. Web Intelligence*, 658–661. DOI: 10.1109/WI.2003.1241290 Cited on page(s) 11

W. Wu, C. Yu, A. Doan and W. Meng (2004) An interactive clustering-based approach to integrating source query interfaces on the deep Web. In *Proc. ACM SIGMOD Int. Conf. on Management of Data*, 95–106. DOI: 10.1145/1007568.1007582 Cited on page(s) 30, 69, 74, 75, 79, 94, 111

P. Wu, J.-R. Wen, H. Liu and W.-Y. Ma (2006a) Query selection techniques for efficient crawling of structured Web sources. In *Proc. International Conference on Data Engineering*, paper 47. DOI: 10.1109/ICDE.2006.124 Cited on page(s) 11, 13, 31, 46, 49, 51, 74, 90, 94

W. Wu, A. Doan and C. Yu (2006b) WebIQ: Learning from the Web to match deep-Web query interfaces. In *Proc. 22nd Int. Conf. on Data Engineering*, paper 44. DOI: 10.1109/ICDE.2006.172 Cited on page(s) 13, 26, 53

W. Wu, A. Doan, C. Yu and W. Meng (2009) Modeling and extracting deep-Web query interfaces. In Z. W. Ras and W. Ribarsky, Eds., *Advances in Information and Intelligent Systems*, 65–90. Springer. DOI: 10.1007/978-3-642-04141-9_4 Cited on page(s) 23, 24, 29, 30, 33

H. Xu, C. Zhang, X. Hao and Y. Hu (2007a) A machine learning approach classification of deep Web sources. In *Proc. 4th Int. Conf. on Fuzzy Systems and Knowledge Discovery*, 561–565. DOI: 10.1109/FSKD.2007.54 Cited on page(s) 53

H. Xu, X. Hao, S. Wang and Y. Hu (2007b) A method of deep Web classification. In *Proc. 6th Int. Conf. on Machine Learning and Cybernetics*, 4009–4014. DOI: 10.1109/ICMLC.2007.4370847 Cited on page(s) 53, 64

C. Yu and W. Meng (1997) *Principles of Database Query Processing for Advanced Applications*. Morgan Kaufmann Publishers. Cited on page(s) 96, 98, 113, 114

Y. Zhai and B. Liu (2006) Structured data extraction from the Web based on partial tree alignment. *IEEE Trans. Knowl. and Data Eng.* 18(12), 1614–1628. DOI: 10.1109/TKDE.2006.197 Cited on page(s) 14

Z. Zhang, B. He and K. Chang (2004) Understanding Web query interfaces: Best-effort parsing with hidden syntax. In *Proc. ACM SIGMOD Int. Conf. on Management of Data*, 107–118. DOI: 10.1145/1007568.1007583 Cited on page(s) 12, 24, 30, 32, 33, 56, 111

Z. Zhang, B. He and K. C.-C. Chang (2005) Light-weight domain-based form assistant: Querying web databases on the fly. In *Proc. 31st Int. Conf. on Very Large Data Bases*, 97–108. Cited on page(s) 18

M. Zhang, N. Zhang and G. Das (2011) Mining enterprise search engine's corpus: Efficient yet unbiased sampling and aggregate estimation. In *Proc. ACM SIGMOD Int. Conf. on Management of Data*, 793–804. DOI: 10.1145/1989323.1989406 Cited on page(s) 31, 46

H. Zhao, W. Meng, Z. Wu, V. Raghavan and C. Yu (2005) Fully automatic wrapper generation for search engines. In *Proc. 14th Int. World Wide Web Conf.*, 66–75. DOI: 10.1145/1060745.1060760 Cited on page(s) 14

P. Zhao, L. Huang, W. Fang and Z. Cui (2008) Organizing structured deep Web by clustering query interfaces link graph. In *Proc. 4th Int. Conf. on Advanced Data Mining and Applications*, 683–690. DOI: 10.1007/978-3-540-88192-6_72 Cited on page(s) 53

J. Zhu, Z. Nie, J. Wen, B. Zhang and W. Ma (2006) Simultaneous record detection and attribute labeling in Web data extraction. In *Proc. ACM SIGKDD Conference*, 494–503. DOI: 10.1145/1150402.1150457 Cited on page(s) 15

P. M. Zillman (2012) *Deep Web Research 2012*. Available at `http://www.deepwebresearch.info/`. Accessed on May 29, 2012. Cited on page(s) 1, 3

Authors' Biographies

EDUARD C. DRAGUT

Eduard C. Dragut is currently a Postdoctoral Research Associate at Purdue University, Discovery Park, Cyber Center. He completed his Ph.D. degree in Computer Science from University of Illinois at Chicago in July 2010. His Ph.D. research focused on the integration of deep Web sources that provide/sell similar products/services. His research interests include databases, information retrieval, managing unstructured data, information extraction, opinion mining and retrieval, and Web data management. Projects he is actively pursuing include deep Web integration systems, online record linkage and fusion, large-scale entity disambiguation, creation of a sentiment word dictionary, and recently, cyber-infrastructure for scientific research.

WEIYI MENG

Weiyi Meng is currently a professor in the Department of Computer Science of the State University of New York at Binghamton. He received his Ph.D. in Computer Science from University of Illinois at Chicago in 1992. In the same year, he joined his current department as a faculty member. He is a co-author of two books "Principles of Database Query Processing for Advanced Applications" and "Advanced Metasearch Engine Technology." He has published over 120 papers. He has served as general chair and program chair of several international conferences and as program committee members of over 50 international conferences. He is on the editorial boards of the World Wide Web Journal, the Frontiers of Computer Science journal, and a member of the Steering Committee of the WAIM conference series. In recent years, his research has focused on metasearch engines, Web data integration, Internet-based Information Retrieval, information extraction, sentiment analysis, and information truthfulness and trustworthiness. He has done pioneering work in large-scale metasearch engines. He was a co-founder of an Internet company (Webscalers) and served as its president. Webscalers developed the world's largest news metasearch engine AllInOneNews.

CLEMENT T. YU

Clement T. Yu is a professor of computer science at the University of Illinois at Chicago. His research interests include multimedia information retrieval, metasearch engine, database management, and applications to healthcare. He has published more than 200 papers in these areas and he is a co-author of two books "Principles of Database Query Processing for Advanced Applications" and "Advanced Metasearch Engine Technology." He served as chairman of the ACM SIGIR and has extensive experience as a consultant in the fields of query processing in distributed and heterogeneous environments, including document retrieval. He was an advisory committee member for the National Science Foundation and was on the editorial boards of IEEE Transactions on Knowledge and Data Engineering, the Journal of Distributed and Parallel Databases, the International Journal of Software Engineering and Knowledge Engineering, and WWW: Internet and Web Information Systems. He also served as the General Chair of the ACM SIGMOD Conference and Program Committee Chair of the ACM SIGIR Conference. He is a co-founder of two Internet companies, Webscalers and PharmIR.